TIPS OF THE TRADE FROM A PRO

Do the right thing—with the right kind of help from an interior design pro! Discover:

- ❀ Why it's vital that you learn the elements of basic construction
- ❀ Foolproof suggestions for choosing wallpaper—and finding the colors, patterns, and textures that are perfect for you and the room
- ❀ The best rooms in which to experiment with strong colors and patterns
- ❀ The single most important piece of advice to follow *before* buying furniture
- ❀ How to find the right upholstering professional—and seven questions you must ask in order to get what you want
- ❀ The differences between soft and hard window treatments— and the four basic elements to any soft window treatment
- ❀ Why the single most important element in any window treatment is the installer

Everything you need to know is here, in one handy volume chock-full of essential information about home decorating: money-saving tips, headache-sparing musts, helpful checklists, shopping notes, and which questions to ask. You, too, can learn to decorate like a pro with this easy-to-use, must-have guide. . . .

My Name Isn't Martha, But I Can Decorate My Home

The Real Person's Guide to
Creating a Beautiful Home
Easily and Affordably

My Name Isn't Martha, But I Can Decorate My Home

Sharon Hanby-Robie

POCKET BOOKS
New York   London   Toronto   Sydney   Tokyo   Singapore

For orders other than by individual consumers, Pocket Books grants a discount on the purchase of **10 or more** copies of single titles for special markets or premium use. For further details, please write to the Vice-President of Special Markets, Pocket Books, 1633 Broadway, New York, NY 10019-6785, 8th Floor.

For information on how individual consumers can place orders, please write to Mail Order Department, Simon & Schuster Inc., 200 Old Tappan Road, Old Tappan, NJ 07675.

An *Original* Publication of POCKET BOOKS

POCKET BOOKS, a division of Simon & Schuster Inc.
1230 Avenue of the Americas, New York, NY 10020

Copyright © 1998 by Starburst Publishers

Interior illustrations by Melissa Burkhart

ISBN: 0-671-01542-7

First Pocket Books trade paperback printing February 1998

10 9 8 7 6 5 4 3 2

POCKET and colophon are registered trademarks of
Simon & Schuster Inc.

Cover design by Jeanne M. Lee
Cover photo credits: author by Steven Skoll; scissors, frame and
tape measure courtesy of Photodisc
Text design by Stanley S. Drate and Ellen Gleeson/Folio Graphics Co. Inc.

Printed in the U.S.A.

ACKNOWLEDGMENTS

My many thanks to all the clients who have inspired me and allowed me to be part of their homes. I am also thankful for the wisdom and creativity of the fine craftsmen, seamstresses, and artists who made the expression of dreams a reality.

I thank my mother, who said, "Whatever it is, you can do it."

Thanks to all my friends for their support and prayers.

Special thanks to my husband, Dave, whose undaunted faith and encouragement is a constant source of love and support.

Praise and glory to God, the inspiration of all beauty.

CONTENTS

EXPLANATION OF ICONS

Throughout the book, there are many useful asides meant to guide, give caution, suggest ideas, and provide advice and pertinent information. These sidebars are divided into the following four categories:

 TRICKS OF THE TRADE—Advice and inside information about the world of home decorating, revealing industry secrets on how to cut costs, discover hard-to-find bargains, and much more.

 FISTFUL OF DOLLARS—Facts and figures you need to know in order to stay on budget and save mounds of money while decorating your home.

 IDEAS AND TRENDS—Like your own personal interior designer, these sidebars will suggest helpful hints on the latest in decor, fashion, and selecting the perfect styles to suit your own tastes.

 BE FOREWARNED—Essential cautions on how to sidestep pitfalls, avoid getting ripped off, and be prepared for every decorating contingency that may arise.

INTRODUCTION

Just for the record, I would not have written this book if I thought it would cost me my job. I do recognize that there will always be people who will never use an interior designer, and others who will always use professionals. My goal is to help you become more informed so you can make wise choices.

Other than the actual cost of your home, the greatest expenditure you make will probably be for its furnishings. Most important, our homes and the atmosphere we create in them affect how we feel, act, and respond to life. Home is where we go for comfort, rest, assurance, and inspiration. Creating an interior design that will make your home look great, meet the needs of your lifestyle, reflect your personality, all while staying in your budget, is hard work indeed.

As a designer, I always consider this challenge to be my most important job. Design school emphasizes that we are problem solvers. And budget problems are certainly an issue designers are used to dealing with. I believe the smaller the budget, the more a designer is needed. Small budgets leave no room for mistakes. It is important to get a clear idea of the big picture before you start making decisions, and a designer can help you do this.

In my twenty-plus years as an interior designer, I've come to recognize that the most important tool is knowledge. The goal of this book is to provide you with a resource to gain that knowledge. Whether you choose to ask for a little professional help or to go it alone, remember—half the fun is in the doing. Enjoy the ride!

My Name Isn't Martha, But I Can Decorate My Home

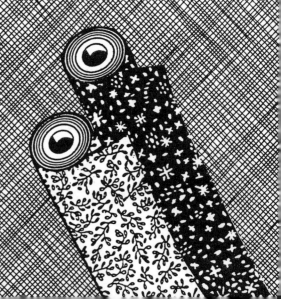

THE BASICS

Let's start at the beginning. The first question usually asked by a designer or salesperson is, What are you looking for? Unfortunately, most people cannot answer this question. This is because we generally know what we *don't* like, not what we *do* like. And many of us don't really know what will fit or work in our rooms.

I usually begin with basic questions designed to get you thinking about the practical nature of the space you are decorating, such as:

* How will this room be used and by whom?
* Do you have pets? What color are they? (*Never* purchase dark-colored furniture if you have a white dog or cat!)
* Do you have children? How old are they?
* Will there be a television in this room?
* Is the room sunny or dark?
* Do you read a lot?
* Do you like playing games or putting puzzles together?
* What kind of crafts do you enjoy?
* Do you have any hobbies?
* Are you a collector? What do you collect? Do you want it displayed? Should it be in a locked cabinet?
* Do you prefer stripes or floral patterns?
* Do you like wallpaper?
* Are you a tailored kind of person?
* How organized are you? How organized would you like to be?

- How long will you be living in this home?
- Are you planning any major changes in your life? Retirement? Children?
- Do you entertain a lot? In what way?

Quite a diverse list of questions, right? Well, the list does go on even further. But I think you get the point. And at least it gets you thinking in the right direction about which factors you will need to take into consideration so that your home will both reflect your overall style and accommodate your life.

But nothing regarding style is set in stone. For example, if you prefer tailored styling, are organized, like dark rich shades and mahogany wood, it would be a good bet that you would prefer heavily carved, formal Eighteenth-Century furniture over the simple clean lines of contemporary furniture. By answering these questions, your personal style will begin to become clear to you.

Sometimes, we like a "little" traditional with our contemporary; a mixture of styles like this is known as *eclectic*. Imagine the clean simple look of a rich mahogany wall system, with the sleek lines of a tailored leather sofa, combined with one wonderful, large and ornately carved Georgian-style desk. Now surround this with deep-pumpkin textured walls—you get a tasteful combination of different styles that work together as a whole. Eclectic can be the best of both worlds.

The Ink Blot Test

The second phase of this exploration of your tastes is what I call my Ink Blot Test. Over the years, I have found this to be the most helpful and insightful way to discover your personal style. The test itself seems simple, but the amount of information you will obtain from it will amaze you.

My second meeting with a client usually takes place at my studio. I use the information I gathered from my questions and combine them with what I learned about the client's personality and home at our first meeting. I then begin to assemble the Ink Blot.

The Ink Blot is actually a sampling of several different styles and colors of wallpaper and fabric that I usually pull from many sources. I show these samples one at a time to my clients and ask their opinion about each one. The clients usually say, "Where are you thinking of putting that?" I assure them that I wasn't thinking of putting it anywhere. You see, I'm not selecting these samples for them. My intent is to just get their true reaction. The idea is to look at many different ideas and to say Yes or No to each.

I've used this little test for nearly twenty years, and it has held up to the test of time. The colors, pattern styles, and textures that you have a positive emotional response to will always appeal to you. Here's how you do it:

STEP ONE—COMPILING THE PILE

I suggest you go to a wallpaper store and just start looking at sample books. It is important that you look at patterns and styles that you normally avoid. The point is to get a wider perspective of what is available. By expanding your horizon, you will further develop your sense of style. Just because you always *thought* you were straight-laced traditional, doesn't necessarily mean you are. It may be that you've chosen a traditional style because it's all you've known.

Start making a stack of samples. Put the "Yes, I like that—I'm not sure for where, but I like it" patterns in the Yes stack. After about an hour of looking, you will be pleasantly surprised to realize that there are similarities among your choices. Usually either color, pattern, or overall personality will be very much the same from one Yes sample to the next. You may, for example, find that many of the samples you have chosen are plaid. They will also have similar colors. They may be different hues (shades), but usually fall within the same color families, like warm or cool colors.

STEP TWO—ANALYZING THE COLORS

In using the Ink Blot Test, I have found that the world is basically divided into two groups, *blue people* and *green people*. The majority of men seem to be blue people. And probably only 30 percent of all people are green people. What this means is that if you were given a choice between blue and green, you would have a definite opinion of which you prefer. Blue people tend to be happier with peach, mauve, gray, beige, rust, and brown tones. Green people prefer brighter, more adventurous tones, such as purple, red, yellow, teal, and hot pink. Yes, you may like both blue and green, but you will generally find that if you are a blue person, the shades of green that appeal to you have blue undertones. It is possible for blue and green people to like the same patterns, but in different color combinations. For the most part, blue people prefer calmer, less radical patterns. Green people often like things with more zing! An example of a "true blue" color combination is yellow, blue, orange, and white, as in Portuguese chinaware. A "true green" color combination is green, red, cream, and white, as in the Alexander Julian *Home Colours* collection. Again, it is the complementary nature or combination of the overall color scheme that defines blue versus green. Are the colors you like bright or soft? Are they strong or subtle in "feeling"? This will tell a lot about your own personal style. It is important to keep the hue or shade (strength or paleness) of the colors in balance. A really strong red would not balance with a very pale yellow. The intensity of each color must be at the same level.

STEP THREE—ANALYZING THE STYLE

Okay, so now you have a pile of swatches that appeal to you. What's next? Well, first recognize the elements of the styles you have chosen. Are they formal, such as silks and brocade patterns? Or are they informal with rough-textured weaves? Determining the level of formality that appeals to you will make it easier to arrange your room. Formal style dictates a more symmetrically balanced plan. Informal is just that: less defined, with fewer rules—more casual. Shopping for furniture will also be a lot easier if you know what style to begin looking at. Obviously, if what you have chosen is formal and softer in color, this is the direction in which you should continue to go.

Look at the wallpaper and fabric samples carefully. Are they representative of traditional or contemporary style? Some patterns can be used for either style, but generally speaking there will be a focus to your selections in one direction or the other. If you find you have chosen several patterns that "feel" as though they could be traditional *or* contemporary, than this may indicate that a combination of styles would be best for you. If you find that all but one of the Yes samples are traditional, don't assume it's a mistake. That's the clue for you to use one contemporary piece of art in your otherwise traditional room. My own personal style is a mixture of French country and contemporary. The truth is, that after being in the design industry for so long, and having acquired such an appreciation for most styles, I would be bored with just one particular style.

STEP FOUR—ANALYZING THE DETAILS

Look at the original samples again and ask yourself, are they busy or simple? Knowing this will give you further insight into your own personal taste. I personally prefer cleaner lines. But as I matured (I hate that word!), I have acquired a taste for more details—hence, my preference for French country style, which has more intricate patterns and ornate designs. I still would not be happy with tons of ribbons, bows, baskets, and an abundance of accessories. The choices you have made in your Yes pile will also give you clues to the kinds of choices you will make in furniture and accessories. If, for example, the samples have a lot of detail, this may indicate that you would like more detailed furniture styles, such as Eighteenth Century or French Provincial (lots of carving and details). If your samples are simpler, you may prefer the minimalist features of Shaker or contemporary styling.

By now, you should be getting a good picture of what appeals to you. Remember, this is based purely on your immediate "emotional" response. *Do not* worry about what anyone else will think. The important thing right now is how you feel about the samples. If you have a housemate, or a whole family of housemates, I would have each one do his or her own Ink Blot Test. Once the preferences of the household members have been established, you can begin to compromise on whose style will dominate and whose will complement. You may even decide to give someone his own room, to do with as he wishes.

Your Choices and Your Walls

PHASE ONE

You have now completed the Ink Blot Test and you've determined your personal style. The next order of business to attend to is to decide exactly what will go where.

What will you do with the walls? Will the sofa be a solid color, or a wonderful floral print, or even a plaid? Start by asking yourself these questions, which will help you to match your choices to the rooms of your home:

❀ Are you a wallpaper person, or would you rather cover your walls with art and accessories?

❀ Did the original samples you selected tend to be nonpattern and just texture? If so, then you may want to consider a tone-on-tone pattern for your large upholstered furniture and use texture or just one color on the walls. You probably should also stay away from a lot of patterns and simply use different shades and tones to create interest. This is a beautiful look, formal and elegant, which can work for both contemporary and traditional rooms. Yes, contemporary can be formal, just as traditional can be informal.

❀ Were the samples all the same color? Then a monochromatic (one-color) scheme will probably suit you best. This can make a powerful statement, particularly when it's accented with great artwork and accessories.

❀ Were the samples you chose bright, with large wonderful patterns? Then it would make sense to use a variety of patterns, with complementing textures. I generally recommend not using more than three dominant colors in one room. You can use many patterns in a room, but they need to be compatible not only in color and style, but in the size of pattern scale as well. For example, if you have chosen a pattern with a large repeat (the size of the pattern) for your first selection, then choose at least one or two more patterns of similar repeat sizes. If your first selection was a floral, then look for plaid, striped, or geometric patterns to work with it. Then you can begin to reduce the size of the repeat in the next two patterns, or add interest with strong texture and color to complement the original choice.

❀ Do you get bored with the way a room looks and want to make changes often? If so, you may want to keep the more expensive items in flexible or neutral colors and patterns.

As you begin to work your way through this list, here are some ideas for consideration.

If you choose a large pattern with strong color on your walls, you will reduce the overall visual space of the room. That's okay. Sometimes that is exactly the effect that you want. If your room is large and feels like a rotunda and your desire is to make it more intimate, then this technique will work perfectly. You can also make a small room become a wonderful theme room by using a large-scale pattern on the walls. You can create a "garden" effect or a "jungle" look using this technique.

If you desire to create a "den" feeling, then warm strong colors will help to accomplish this. Dining rooms are also a good place to try this creative style. Generally, we don't spend as much time in the dining room as we do in most of the rest of the house, so it is wonderful to have an atmosphere that brings intimacy and warmth to meals and gatherings in this room. I painted my last dining room in a rich, warm, red-rust tone. It wasn't something I would have wanted for the living room, but for my dining area it was perfect! Artwork and accessories were done in lighter tones to set off the color. Everyone commented on how nice it was to eat in there!

Before doing an entire room in a strong color, first try doing just one wall. In my last home, I had chosen a deep rich shade of cayenne (rust) for the walls. I was at work when the painter started painting. He had no idea what color the paint was supposed to be. The manufacturer used only numbers to identify the paint, instead of names for color. Well, I got a panic-stricken phone call from the painter at work. He was terrified that he had gotten the number wrong. He had painted two walls before calling and was not certain what to do next. When I arrived, I was thrilled—it was beautiful! And I never tired of that room. It was warm and cozy no matter what time of day, whatever the weather.

Another room for experimenting with strong pattern or color is a powder room or bathroom. Again, because we don't usually "live" in these rooms, it is easier to accept a wild idea. After all, we're just passing through. If, after trying this in a small space, you find you really love it, then go ahead and be brave. Try a larger room.

A foyer or entryway is another one of my favorite spaces to have fun with! I think that this space should be an introduction to what to expect from the rest of the house. It can be used to tie together the rest of your home. Let's say your living room is peach, soft teal, and beige. And your dining room is a deeper shade of peach with soft peach, yellow, and a hint of red. Then you could use a wonderful wallpaper pattern that would incorporate all of these colors for the entry. The scale should be appropriate for the size of the space, but if possible, similar to or larger than the patterns used in the living and dining rooms. After all, it is the opening statement to your home and can therefore be a bit exaggerated. You can use virtually any combination of colors for your home, as long as you find something to tie them together. This can be a piece of artwork, a fabric, wallpaper, or even a carpet—almost anything! I actually have designed homes around one piece of art.

The good news is that if you use the walls to start implementing your color and style, you can always repaint or repaper. However, if you bought a unique patterned sofa first, that commits you to this new and adventurous world. Yes, you can reupholster, but it's a bit more difficult—possible, but a really involved job.

PHASE TWO

With a basic idea of where you want to use the more dominant patterns in your room, you can begin to further define the final choices of color and pattern and to focus on finding complementary samples for the rest of the room. In doing so, you want to give yourself several options to choose from.

This is where most clients get stuck. They find that there are a lot of samples that they now find appealing. You have to get tough with yourself. Look at only two of the new samples and ask yourself the following question: If I could use only one of these, which one would I choose? Then proceed with the same question through the rest of the samples. You *will* find the *one* that you like best—trust me! Recently I saw an old client. He said that there were two things I had taught him. The first was the Ink Blot and the second, to trust me! I laughed, but I think it is much more important to trust yourself. Most people get stuck because they are unsure of themselves and don't want to make a mistake. Learn to trust your instincts—they are your best bet for making good decisions.

Note that some elements of a room will need to be chosen before you have a set plan for your wall finishes. If you plan on using an Oriental carpet in a room, for instance, then choose it first, before selecting any finishes. It is far easier to find a suitable fabric or wallpaper to match a carpet than vice versa.

Once you have determined the basic

style and color for the walls and upholstered furniture, you can begin to choose the artistic elements of your room. Give yourself more freedom when selecting items such as a cocktail table. Think of this not only as a practical item, but a piece of art. Yes, it needs to serve you well, but it is also a great opportunity to "play" a little. Have fun with this. Allow yourself to go over the edge, even if just a little! If your room so far is very traditional, then try a glass and brass version of a French traditional table to add interest and bring a traditional style into the twenty-first century.

Another option for adding surprise to a room is with an interesting *occasional piece*. Occasional furniture is defined as almost any table, cabinet, or accessory furniture, such as a plant stand or baker's rack. If your style is a soft contemporary then you might choose a painted and decorated carved chest as an accent. This is what makes decorating fun! Occasional items do not have to be expensive. They are there for their artistic value, not their practicality.

I'll go into more detail on where to begin and how to proceed in later chapters, but to recap, here are the basics:

1. Take the Ink Blot Test.
2. Select specific fabrics and wall covering finishes.
3. Choose upholstered furniture.
4. Choose hard furniture (table, cabinets, etc.).
5. Choose flooring.
6. Choose the artistic elements—occasional furnishings.
7. Finally, fill in the blanks with accessories. Think of accessories as jewelry for your room. After all, even the perfect little black dress or the most expensive hand-tailored suit needs the balanced finishing touch of appropriate jewelry.

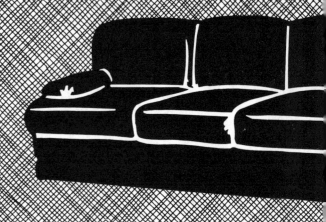

2

WHAT'S THE DIFFERENCE BETWEEN A $399 SOFA AND A $7,000 SOFA?

You're ready to take the big step—you're going to buy a sofa. Is this the first time you're purchasing a sofa? If you are like most of us, even if you have purchased one before, it has probably been a while since your last new sofa. Most people replace their car more often than they replace their sofa. How much are you prepared to spend? Not sure? Most people aren't. Be careful, you may get sticker shock! If you hadn't purchased a car in ten years, you would be mighty surprised at what a new car costs today. The same is true for furniture. After all, it has been escalating in price at the same rate as the price of cars.

Deciding how much to spend requires some knowledge of basic construction and an awareness of how you will actually use your sofa now, as well as in the future. The old adage "You get what you pay for" is very true when it comes to furniture. You *can* find quality furniture, you just have to know what to look for.

Sofa, Love Seat, Sectional, or Modular

When is a sofa not a sofa? Answer: When it is a love seat, sectional, modular, chaise, chair-and-a-half, or a chair!

You probably know what a love seat and a chair are, and if you remember the fifties, then you may know what a sectional is. But if you haven't shopped for a number of years, you may not know what a modular or a chaise is.

A *love seat* is simply a small sofa with seating for two—preferably lovers! A *chair-and-a-half* is a smaller version meant for *really* friendly lovers!

More often than not, I find that a modular or sectional will actually be more appropriate than a sofa because of its versatility. A *modular* is several pieces of a sofa that you can arrange in almost any shape or size you need. It usually consists of end pieces that have one arm, a few armless sections, and either curved or straight corner sections. When you are standing in front of a piece, if the arm is on your right, then it is called a *right-facing piece;* if it is on your left, it is obviously a *left-facing piece*. These are usually the same size as a normal chair. If they are larger and include more than enough room for one person, then they become a *chaise* or *lounge*. Armless pieces are exactly what they sound like—armless. They are also usually one seat wide—if they have two seats, they become *armless love seats*. If they have three or more seats, they are *armless sofas*. *Corner sections* are either square (basically a seat with two backs) or they are curved. The curved corner or wedge-shaped corner is larger and requires more room and depth. If you get a curved corner, you will end up with a "dead space" behind it that is useful only for a floor lamp or a custom-shaped table.

The advantage to a modular is its flexibility. You can create L-shapes and U-shapes and use a variety of shapes and sizes around the room. I personally have not owned a simple love seat or sofa in over twenty years. I knew that I would be doing a lot of moving. So it made sense for me to have something that could be rearranged to fit the needs of each new room.

When purchasing modular furniture, try to anticipate your future needs. If you expect to be moving about a lot in the next several years, I suggest purchasing two corner units, four armless pieces, and one or two ottomans (footstools). This will give you a lot of options for rearranging later on.

Sectionals generally consist of three pieces: a corner and two one-arm sofas that fit together to form an L-shape. The corner can be square or curved. As with modulars, curved corners of sectionals take up more room than square ones, but they provide for a place to put your legs and actually sit, rather than lounge.

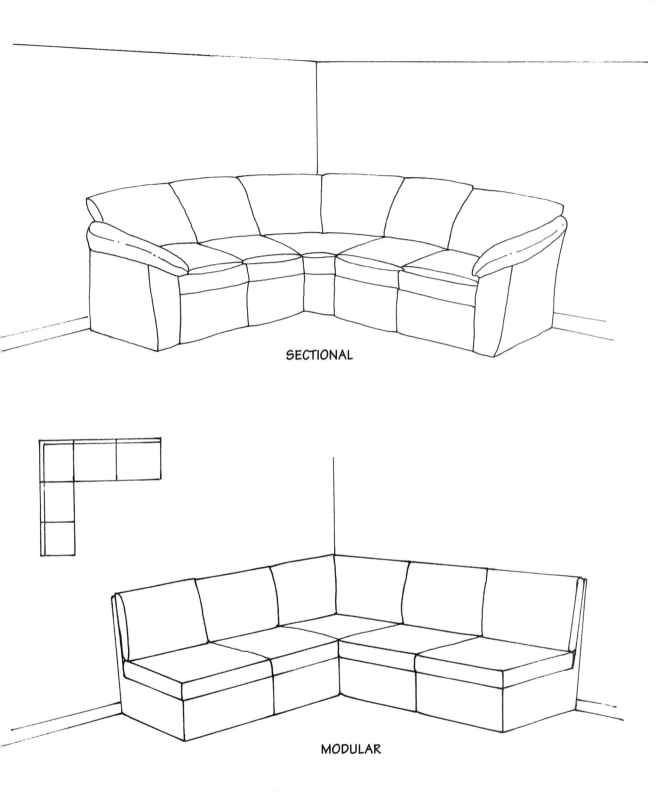

SECTIONAL

MODULAR

What's the Difference Between a $399 Sofa and a $7,000 Sofa? • 13

Construction

SPRINGS

Okay, this may be boring, but it is necessary. It's time to learn some basic construction. The most expensive sofas (or any other piece of upholstered furniture—chair, bench, or whatever) have what are called hand-tied coil springs. They are exactly what they sound like. Imagine several coiled springs. These springs are then tied to each other, and to the frame, at eight different points around the spring's diameter. You now have eight-way hand-tied spring construction! That's the stuff that gives the sofa its bounce—the reason kids like to jump up and down on the sofa! This spring construction is remarkably strong. Once, a client brought in her two teenage children and had them jump up and down on all the sofas in my shop to test the different models. I was horrified! They actually made their decision based on their children's little exercise. I must admit, I hesitated the next time that client called for me to design another room.

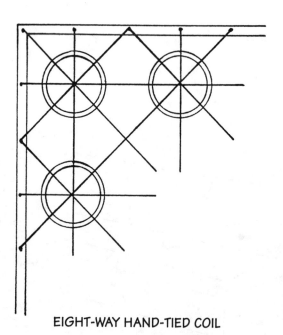

EIGHT-WAY HAND-TIED COIL

The other most-used spring construction is no-sag spring construction. Imagine a snake winding its way across the floor, back and forth. That is pretty much what a no-sag spring looks like. It is a fairly thick wire that has been bent into this shape. The wire is longer than the measurement from the front of the sofa to the back, so that when attached to the front and back of the frame, it creates an arch, thus giving the sofa the bounce or spring action that it needs. Sometimes, this type of construction is used on an expensive sofa to accommodate style, particularly on the more contemporary or modern models.

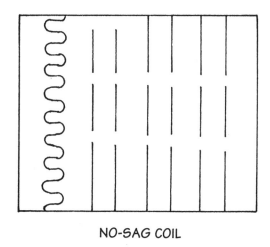

NO-SAG COIL

THE FRAME

The next important item in the expensive sofa is the wood frame. It makes sense that hardwoods are most desirable. But there are different kinds of wood classified as hard, such as oak, maple, and mahogany. And though it may be great hardwood, has it been kiln dried? It makes a difference. Kiln drying is a process that removes excess moisture and sap from the wood. You don't want the frame to start warping and bending because it wasn't properly dried.

The construction techniques of the frame are also very important. Does it have glued or screwed corner blocks? These are little blocks of wood used to support the corner joints of the frame. Sometimes they are glued in place, sometimes they are screwed in place, and other times both techniques are used.

Other factors also come into play. When you sit on the front edge of the sofa, does it have any give? Lift up the seat cushion and press on the front edge of the sofa. An expensive or well-made sofa will have a spring set into the front edge, allowing for flex.

The padding of the frame is also important. Like testing a tire by giving it a kick, there are some places on a sofa to "kick" as well. Feel the outside arm of the sofa. Does it push right in? Or is there some padding behind it? You want to make sure it is reasonably taut. You don't want the side of the sofa to collapse if the kids run up and fall into it. The same is true for the back of the sofa. Don't expect a hard surface behind it, as most sofas don't have one, but it should at least have some support. The amount of padding on the top of the arm is also an important aspect. Arms are subject to a lot of abuse. If there is not sufficient padding, the fabric will wear out much faster.

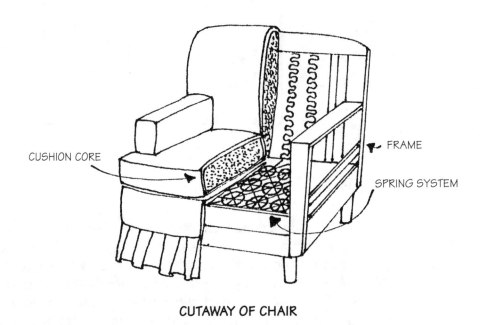

CUSHION CORE

FRAME

SPRING SYSTEM

CUTAWAY OF CHAIR

CUSHIONS

Cushions are a *very* important feature. The stuffing in the cushions is what will determine how your sofa will look after five thousand seatings! There is also a difference between the seat and back cushions. They serve quite different purposes.

Seat Cushions

The seats need to have a firm foundation—either springs or a urethane foam core is best. Your preference in firmness levels will determine what is most appropriate for you. Generally speaking, more expensive sofas have coil foundations. If a foam core is used, the density of the foam will make a difference in the life of the cushion. The next item of importance is the wrapping, which may consist of cotton, cotton-fiber batting, feathers (duck or goose down—this should be encased in a down-proof ticking), or polyester-fiber batting.

The top side of the seat cushion has a *crown*. A crown is a curve or a slight arching on the top. The higher the crown, the better the cushion should wear.

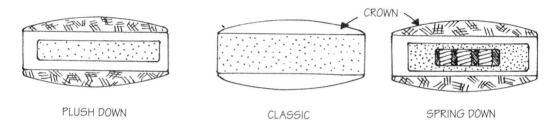

PLUSH DOWN   CLASSIC   SPRING DOWN

TYPES OF SEAT CUSHIONS

Back Cushions

The back cushions do not have the firm foundation that the seat cushions have. Rather than coils, a foam core is usually the firmest foundation used. But again, this really is more a preference than anything else. The more expensive sofa back cushions consist of down feathers with a small foam core. They feel wonderful, but they do need fluffing after every use! The most popular back cushion construction is a foam core wrapped in poly batting or shredded foam. The least expensive sofa may have back cushions made entirely out of shredded foam. These cushions will not hold their shape as well and will soon resemble lumpy squashed blobs.

ARM COVERS

An expensive sofa will have arm covers available free of charge. However, if you want a complete arm sleeve, you will need to pay extra. So what's the difference? Arm covers, or arm caps, cover just about one-third of the exposed arm. Arm sleeves cover the entire arm from front to back, and also down the inside to the seat. It takes much more fabric for this item—hence the cost. Arm covers of any sort do make a difference, but only if you use them!

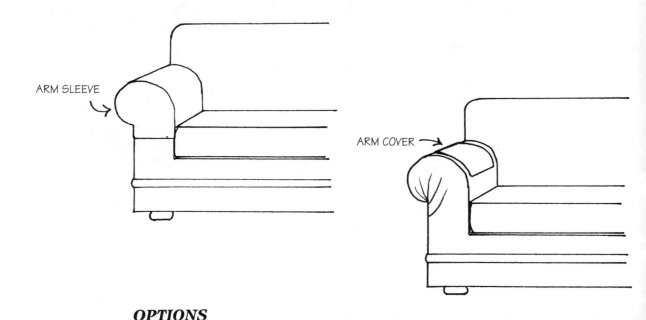

ARM SLEEVE

ARM COVER

OPTIONS

Options, options, options. These can really make a difference in the cost of a sofa. The less-expensive sofa will have no options available to you. The expensive one will allow you to customize your sofa to fit your needs. Examples include size by the inch, the style of the arm, the height of the arm, the height of the seat, the height of the back, attached or detached back cushions, the firmness of the cushions, the style of the skirt or base, the color of stain on the legs or feet (even if you can't see them because of the skirt)—the list is endless.

So, which ones really matter? It depends! I'll discuss making the right choice later in this chapter, once you know the rest of the elements involved in the construction of sofas.

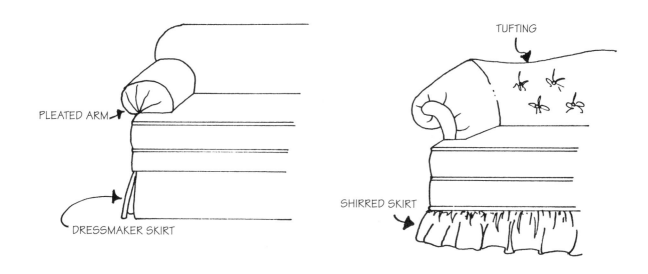

PLEATED ARM

DRESSMAKER SKIRT

TUFTING

SHIRRED SKIRT

Fabric

Fabric—it is probably the most important part of the sofa. What you put around the outside is what you will live with for a very long time. And how this will look after five thousand seatings will determine how happy you will be with your sofa in the future.

Again, options come into play. The less expensive the sofa, the fewer choices you have. And the more expensive, the more choices. And if this is not enough, there is a fabric option known as COM (customer's own material)—better known as "custom fabric," the interior designer's secret weapon! Trust me, once you have been shown the "unavailable except for megabucks fabric," you will have a very difficult time settling for anything else. So my advice is to look at custom fabrics only as a last resort. You may purchase COM fabric anywhere you like. However, if you do not purchase it from the same place that you are buying the sofa from, the sofa's manufacturer will not give a warranty for it.

A few words on COM—when selecing COM fabric, be aware of the size, type, and direction of the pattern. How the pattern is woven and the way it pulls off the bolt will determine which way it will be applied to the sofa. For example, if it's a stripe and it is woven side to side, in a continuous length as you pull it off the bolt, then you need to be sure the sofa manufacturer is informed not to railroad the fabric.

Railroading means applying the fabric side to side, as opposed to up and down. If you railroad a stripe that is woven side to side, you will end up with the stripes going around and around your sofa. And, just as with a dress, it is preferable that the stripes run up and down, not side to side!

Tailoring the fabric will make or break the way your sofa looks. Less expensive sofas will not necessarily have the pattern of the fabric matched. In other words, the stripes may not line up evenly. On a more expensive sofa, the craftsman will, for example, repeat the same flower in the center of each cushion, as opposed to randomly applying the pattern. If you want the arms, skirt, and seats to be pattern-matched properly, you will pay more. For obvious reasons, it requires more fabric and takes more time to lay out the pattern. So your own need for detail will determine how much you will pay for a sofa.

In choosing a fabric, you must be realistic about your lifestyle now and in the future. If this is your first time actually purchasing a sofa, and you plan on using it in your living room until you own a family

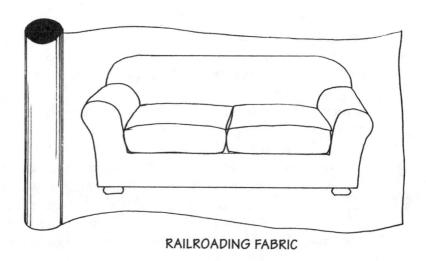

RAILROADING FABRIC

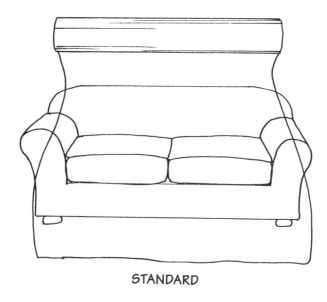

STANDARD

room, when it will become the family room sofa, then there will be different considerations to think about. For example, don't expect to reupholster the sofa later unless it is a really expensive sofa to begin with. The cost will just not be worth it. So in choosing a fabric, be sure that it will be appropriate for a family room full of children, pets, and pizza.

The most important factors in choosing fabric are content, construction, and color.

CONTENT

Technology changes constantly, so there are always new and improved fibers that most of us have never heard of. Some fibers you may be familiar with already are nylon and polyester. These man-made plastic fibers are very durable—not necessarily pleasant, but they do stand up to the test of time. For a family room, I usually recommend a blend with at least 20 percent man-made plastic.

Cotton, wool, and linen are all wonderful natural fibers. Their durability will be dependent upon the type of construction used to produce the fabric.

CONSTRUCTION

A fine weave will usually mean a thinner fabric, like a cotton print or chintz (glazed or polished cotton) for example. Cotton prints are wonderful, but not very durable. I recommend using them in parlors (or any room you almost never use!).

Velvets are actually quite hardy. They usually are 100 percent cotton, but some manufacturers add a little polyester or nylon, which helps to make the fabric stronger. A little texture in velvets improves their ability to hide all the pizza sauce and butter from the popcorn. I have seen cotton velvets survive the "war of the family room" for as long as ten years!

Herculon (meant to sound like Hercules) is a disaster fabric. The concept was great, but the weave of the construction was much too loose; as a result, it completely unravels like a cheap sweater with a pull. Again, technology is improving, but I am not yet convinced that all the bugs have been worked out of this one.

There are a lot of fabrics that resemble Herculon, only they are much better. Nylon, polyester, and blends of many fibers woven into bulky, multicolored textures are really great for durability and soil-hiding capability.

Linen can be expensive! Wonderful for its look, feel, and emotional impact, unfortunately, linen does not hold color well. It will eventually look worn out on all the parts where friction occurs (the edges, corners, arms, etc.). It won't *actually* be worn out, it's just that the color will have rubbed off.

I think denim is a great fabric. Someone finally figured out that if we like to wear denim jeans, we probably wouldn't mind sitting on it, either. It's natural and durable, and the more aged it looks, the better we like it.

Leather has become very popular in the last several years, and with good reason. Leather is durable, cleans easily, and gives you a feeling of luxury. Yes, it may be a bit more expensive, but it is definitely worth it. You will find a lot of options with leather, and as a result, a lot of different price ranges. The less expensive the leather, the thinner it is, and the more imperfections it has. Glove leather is soft, pretty, and very expensive, but not necessarily the most durable. Cowhide is very durable, and a much thicker, stiffer material—more appropriate for casual styles. One of the more recent leather styles is an untanned, almost suedelike finish. It is gorgeous, but be aware that even your "figure-prints" will leave a mark. The more it is used, the more worn or marked it becomes, giving the impression of a very old bomber jacket.

I often recommend leather. It can be repaired if damaged, cut, or scraped with a little kit that includes color for custom dyeing and a gel-like mending product. It works quite well. A leather sofa will easily survive the five-thousand-seating test. People often say leather is cold, which is not exactly true. Leather takes on the temperature of the room it's in, and air temperature is actually cooler than we realize. Leather also gets very warm if it happens to be sitting in a window with the sun beating down on it. Overall, most people find leathers very comfortable.

COLOR

I can't imagine a world without color. This is the one thing I would never, ever try to select for a client. It is so personal. But what's amazing is that most people are dumbfounded when it comes to choosing color for their home furnishings.

Some have suggested you look at your closet and choose the same color palette for your home as you have for your clothes. I do *not* agree with this. I dress according to how I feel in the morning. And I know a lot of people who do the same. If I am in a purple mood, I wear purple. Yet I do not want to look at a purple sofa for the next ten years!

So this is where the Ink Blot Test I discussed in Chapter 1 really comes into play. By taking the time to expose yourself to lots and lots of colors and patterns, you will begin to discover what is right for you. You really need to take the time to do this because you will live with your color choices for a long, long time.

There are some basic thoughts that I can suggest. There have been numerous studies on the psychology of color and how it affects us both mentally and physically. I will not attempt to explain all of it, but I will give you some ideas for thought.

✤ I had a friend who complained that he had been feeling really tired lately. I had known him since college and it was not his normal personality to be tired and draggy. He had recently purchased a condo and had done his own decorating. He thought he had done all the right things. Actually, he had thought it through more than most people when it came to selecting the colors he would use. He owned a large, white, long-haired Hungarian sheepdog. So the carpeting, sofa, draperies, bedding, and throw rugs were a subtle shade of gray or beige, all very handsome.

But there was only one problem: Dave was being put to sleep by his environment! He desperately needed color to stimulate his brain into action. So we did the obvious, and brightened up the place. Yes, his housekeeping required a lot more vacuuming to keep up with the white dog hair that now showed, but as a result, Dave has a lot more energy.

❀ Certain colors will make you hungry. And the kind of food you crave can actually be controlled by color. Pinks, for example, will make you hungry for sweets. So keep this in mind if you're watching your weight. The brighter the pink, the greater the craving!

❀ Once you've used the Ink Blot technique and determined the colors that appeal to you, you can then begin to look at the practicality of your choice. If you have decided that soft pale green is your favorite, I would suggest using it somewhere else in the room other than on the sofa. Soft pale green will not survive five thousand seatings and still remain a soft pale green. You can have soft pale green draperies, walls, even pillows. But find something darker for the sofa.

❀ Just as the soft pale colors will show dirt, so will the really dark colors. Only the dark colors will show the light-colored dirt instead of the dark-colored dirt.

❀ If this is your first real sofa, I recommend choosing something neutral that will allow you to decorate around it. Trust me—pumpkin orange will become very difficult to work with five years from now. The same is true of very busy patterns. It makes much more sense to use busy patterns on the less expensive items in the room. That way when you tire of them, you won't feel so guilty replacing them.

❀ Certain colors last longer. Blues are terrible. They fade and fade. Brown will also lose color very quickly. Did you know it only takes twenty-four continuous hours of exposure to the sun to remove color from a fabric? If a room has a sun exposure of just two hours each day, it will not take long to total twenty-four hours. You will be amazed at what will happen to the color in your sofa, carpet, and draperies. Be careful!

While we're on the subject of color, did you know that there is actually a Color Council that determines which colors will be popular? Surprised? Most people are when they first hear about the Color Council, but it makes sense once you think about it. Can you imagine the chaos if the different components of the home fashions industry were left up to their own whims? You would never be able to get the flooring to match the paint, the wallpaper, or the kitchen sink for that matter! So the Color Council appoints members each year who decide the direction of color for the entire industry. A color, if popular, will have a life span of about seven years. On the other hand, if a color is like a bad movie and gets lousy reviews, it will be gone just as quickly as the bad movie. At least movies have an afterlife—video. Colors do not! That means that if you were the only one in love with the flamingo pink carpet, you will be stuck with it and *never* will be able to find another item to match it.

CLEANING CODES

A national standard Cleanability Code has been established. Unfortunately, this information is generally not shown anywhere on a fabric sample. You will, however, be able to ask your salesperson to locate this information in the manufacturer's fabric list.

There is a disclaimer that all manufacturers apply to these codes. In other words, they will not take responsibility for the effects of cleaning, even if you follow recommended methods.

Here is the disclaimer:

The following recommended cleaning codes are devised as the results of tests made by the fabric manufacturers having adhered to the methods requested by the Joint Upholstery Standards Committee. They in no way intend to imply that we are in any way guaranteeing these fabrics or the cleanability thereof.

The Cleanability Code assigns letters to signify the proper method of cleaning:

W: Clean this fabric only with the foam of a water-based cleaning agent to remove overall soil. Many household cleaning solvents are harmful to the color and life of the fabric. Cleaning only by a professional furniture cleaning service is recommended. To prevent overall soiling, frequent vacuuming or light brushing to remove dust and grime is recommended.

S: Clean this fabric with pure solvents (petroleum distillate-based products like Energine, Carbona, and Renuzit may be used) in a well-ventilated room. Cleaning only by a professional furniture cleaning service is recommended. Caution: water stains may become permanent and are unable to be removed with solvent cleaning agents. Avoid products containing carbon tetrachloride, as it is highly toxic. To prevent overall soiling, frequent vacuuming or light brushing to remove dust and grime is recommended.

SW: Clean this fabric only with the foam of a water-based cleaning agent or with a pure solvent in a well-ventilated room (petroleum distillate-based products like Energine, Carbona, and Renuzit may be used). Cleaning by a professional furniture cleaning service is recommended. To prevent overall soiling, frequent vacuuming or light brushing to remove dust and grime is recommended.

X: Clean this fabric only by vacuuming or light brushing to prevent accumulation of dust or grime. The foam of water-based agents or solvent-based cleaning agents of any kind may cause excessive shrinking or fading.

FABRIC WARRANTIES

Unfortunately, *there are no guarantees for fabric!* No one warrants them for durability, cleanability, or any other quality. The only thing that you can expect is that the fabric will be the fabric you ordered, and it will be cut from the same dye lot.

Measurements

Your own size, height, weight, and width do make a difference. Every sofa has its own unique seating. If you are tall, you will need a deeper seat to accommodate your legs. If you are tall and lean, you will

Be sure to ask for inside seating dimensions. Most manufacturers do not publish this information, but it is available. If you are ordering a sofa from a picture in a catalog, have your salesperson call the factory and get the measurement for you. Experiment with different proportions and firmness levels until you are sure what is best for you.

probably want a softer seat. If you are tall and husky, I suggest a firmer seat to give you better support. The height of the seat will also be important. The taller and older you are, the higher the seat should be. Your width and the width of your family members will determine how long the sofa should be. But be careful here as the measurement given for the length of a sofa also includes the arms. If the arms are lalapaloozas of 15 inches, you lose 30 inches of seating area. The same is true of the depth (front to back) of the sofa. This measurement includes the frame and cushions.

Making the Right Choice

You are now reasonably educated and ready to go stalk the perfect sofa. So how do you actually make that choice?

Before you begin shopping, go back to Chapter 1 and answer the questions that I've listed. You will then be able to determine just how much construction quality will be necessary for this particular room. Be honest with yourself. If your lifestyle includes children in the living room with toys, pets, and friends, don't be unrealistic and expect that just because you've decided to buy a new sofa, everyone will adopt a new lifestyle and be considerate of the new furniture. It won't happen and you will become a raving lunatic trying to make it happen!

If, on the other hand, the room will probably be used only on a few occasions a year, or only for your own personal reading pleasure, then by all means find the prettiest sofa that you find comfortable to sit in for the cheapest price. Speaking of sitting, why is it that when people shop for furniture they act as if they are sitting on Aunt Jane's formal antique settee? Don't just sit in the center of the sofa—act as you do at home. If you have to, take off your shoes, plop in the corner, and slouch. If this is how you will be sitting at home, be sure it is comfortable that way in the store. If you like to lie down, by all means, lie down. There is nothing worse than getting the sofa home and finding out its arms are too high to allow you to lie down comfortably. Buy furniture for you and your family, not the neighbors or Aunt Jane.

I personally have never spent a fortune on a sofa. I would be sick to death of looking at the same sofa for fifteen years, so I do not want a sofa that will last forever. I want to buy a new one when I'm sick of this one! But I am not you. You must decide for yourself what is best for your personality and family.

Always take home a sample of the fabric you are considering and move it around the room. If the sample provided by the manufacturer is too small to give a good idea of how the sofa will look, then spend the money to pay for half a yard of the fabric, if necessary. You will live with this purchase for a long time, so be smart about choosing patterns.

Do not put little tiny dots on a very large sectional. It will make you dizzy.

Catalog shopping is a normal routine in the furniture industry. If you haven't shopped in a while, you may find this alarming, especially after all I've said with regard to comfort and construction. However, I have probably sold more sofas from catalogs than from samples in the showroom. I eventually limited my inventory to only two manufacturers' sofa lines and I know their quality and options very well. Twice a year, I visit the manufacturers' showrooms and sit in all the newest models so I can confidently tell my clients how a sofa or a chair actually sits. Most retailers maintain samples of the different types of cushions offered by a manufacturer. This will make it easier to determine what is best for you. And you can be sure the quality within a particular line of furniture will be consistent.

Be smart—window-shop, browse, take your time. This is not a race so do not give yourself some ridiculous deadline (like a birthday, holiday, or wedding). You will end up regretting decisions made in haste. And remember that every piece of furniture that has to be ordered for you is *not* returnable. It does not matter that the pink and yellow welts on the purple ottoman don't look like what you thought

One of my staff actually allowed a client to custom order an ottoman in neon yellow with hot pink jumbo welts (trim)! All I could say when it came in was, "Ahhhhh!" Unfortunately, the client's response was exactly the same. It looked like it should be on the Pee-Wee Herman show. What a mess!

they would look like—you will still have to pay for it even if you refuse to accept delivery!

Wait for sales! The furniture industry always has a sale on the horizon. It may be after Christmas or around Memorial Day, but there *will* be a sale. Take advantage. But be sure that you have shopped for prices before the sales. Sometimes a sale isn't really a sale. After all, increasing prices on January 1 and having a sale on January 10 is a real possibility.

Take the time to find a salesperson or designer that you trust. These people have an incredible amount of information that will benefit you and can save you lots and lots of money. Most retail furniture stores provide free interior design services, if you are purchasing. However, there is a difference between a designer and a decorator. Most decorators do not have a degree in design, while most designers *do.* Also, note that though the service is free, it does not mean that you are stuck with the first person who approaches you. If there are personality conflicts, do not continue to work with the person. There is nothing she can do that will make you happy, no matter how talented she is. Go to management and explain that you would like to work with someone else. Retail stores use a rotation system for the salespeople/designers. The reason for this is that they are on commission. The system is actually a fair way to work with a commissioned sales staff. But unfortunately, it means that the buyer doesn't get to interview the person he is supposed to spend the big bucks with, and whose advice he is to heed. You do have a choice—use it!

The most important advice I can give is measure *everything.* Especially the width of your doorways. It is impossible to get a 42-inch sofa through a 36-inch doorway!

Checklist

☐ Arm heights
☐ Seat heights
☐ Seat depths
☐ Window heights and widths (Do you want your sofa to show through the window? If so, how will the sun affect it?)
☐ Try out sofas in the store
☐ Make a sketch of your room and measure everything!
☐ Doorway sizes
☐ Traffic patterns
☐ Samples of walls, floors, draperies, and furniture colors
☐ Artwork?
☐ TV?
☐ Sleep on any decision

Shopping Notes and Questions

Don't be talked into more than you need.

Be realistic about how long you expect this sofa to last.

Who will be using this sofa?

What kinds of activities will be going on around or on the sofa?

Are you a corner sitter, a sloucher, a lounger, or a sleeper?

How much time will you actually be spending on the sofa?

How long did your last sofa last? Has your lifestyle changed since then?

How old are your pets? (As they age, they develop habits that cannot be controlled and can be very hazardous to the life of your furniture.)

Are you replacing only the sofa, or will you be redoing the whole room?

What is your time frame for completion? Plan ahead so fabrics will match and wear out at the same time.

Realize that once you replace anything in a room, it may make everything else look old and tattered.

If you have been living with an empty room, it will seem crowded even with only one piece of furniture.

Don't panic when the furniture is delivered—I tell clients that I will not take calls from them for at least forty-eight hours after delivery— you need time to adjust to the changes. We all do!

Words of Wisdom

When a salesperson tells you something has a "lifetime" guarantee—ask whose lifetime it refers to. There's yours and the furniture's. And if it is the furniture's lifetime, then how will you know when its life is over? Hmm. . . .

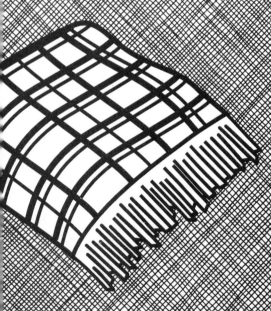

SHOULD I REUPHOLSTER, SLIPCOVER, OR BUY NEW?

Reupholstering

It sounds simple—just change the fabric on the sofa. Get rid of the old, put on the new, and voila—a new sofa! Saves time, money, and the hassle of shopping. Well, it's *not* that simple. First of all, it won't save you time—you will have to shop, order, and wait for fabric, and so on. And only after the fabric has arrived will the workroom put you on their schedule. After all, your fabric may get back ordered until the year 2020. The average waiting period, once you are on the schedule, is six weeks. And unfortunately, in most cases reupholstering will not save money. Have I busted your bubble already? Well, you're not alone.

Whenever someone asks me to give them an estimate to reupholster a piece of furniture, I begin with a series of questions.

1. Would you prefer to keep this piece of furniture even if you could afford to buy a new piece?
2. Is this a treasured family heirloom?
3. Is this a unique or unusual piece of furniture?
4. Is this an antique piece that you've spent the last three hundred years looking for?

You see, if your answer to all of the above questions is no, then you probably should not be reupholstering. You might want to buy something new.

What most people don't realize is that if you do the job properly, the cost of redoing an old piece of furniture is usually the same or higher than that of buying a new one.

Why? Well, let me explain.

THE BASICS

Let's use a sofa as an example. First, the old fabric must be removed. Then the stuffing has to be evaluated. In most cases, the cushion stuffing will need to be replaced. As we discussed in Chapter 2, there are many different kinds of cushion stuffing available. And the prices vary a lot. Often some of the padding around the frame will also have to be replaced.

Next, the entire frame must be checked for defects, cracks, weak areas, or rotting. All the corner blocks must be checked. Basically, every item of the frame that we discussed in Chapter 2 must now be examined and evaluated.

Then we start the "spring thing" again! Naturally, all the springs must be checked and retied. Why? Because the law of averages says if I neglect to retie even *one* spring, that spring is guaranteed to pop after the sofa has been put back together!

So far we've only discussed the inside of the sofa. But that is just the beginning.

FABRIC

Here we go again!

Nearly half of the cost involved will be for the fabric you choose. Of course, you do have control over how much you spend per yard of fabric. But why go through all this work and then put cheap fabric on the sofa? After all, the fabric is what will get most of the wear and tear.

Estimating the amount of fabric necessary can get complex. How far do you want the upholstering matched? In other words, if you are using a floral pattern, do you want each cushion to look exactly the same as the next? How do you want the pattern applied? Do you want the blue or the purple flower to be centered on the cushion?

Suppose you're using a stripe. Do you want the stripes on the skirt of the sofa to line up with the stripes on the seat cushions? The extent of pattern matching will determine how much fabric you will need.

How do you want the skirt made? Do you want pleats? If so, do you want them only on the corners, or do you want boxed pleats all around? Maybe you would like the skirt shirred (gathered). You do have the option to make changes in the style of skirt. You can also change the style of the cushions. Or maybe you would like to add tufting. Do you want arm covers or matching throw pillows? Then, of course, comes the trim. This is also the perfect opportunity to add details that the sofa may not have had, for example, brass nail heads, or large cord trim, or even a fringe to the skirt.

While we are discussing fabric, always ask the upholsterer to return any unused fabric. You never know when it will come in handy. Besides, you've paid for it! But many reupholsterers need to be reminded to return any leftovers.

All of these options will add to the amount of fabric required. Fabrics are basically available in two widths: 48 inches and 54 inches. This will also affect the yardage requirements.

Generally speaking, expect to need somewhere between 18 to 21 yards of fabric for an average 84-inch sofa.

Now, do you want your fabric to be treated for stain resistance? Often this is available directly from the fabric manufacturer. If not, the fabric can be professionally treated prior to being applied to your furniture.

THE WORKSHOP

Okay, we've covered the basics of reupholstering. You now know just enough to begin shopping for the right person to do the job. So where do you begin? Start with a few questions.

1. **Always ask to see the reupholsterer's work.** You would be amazed how many sofas start out nice and comfortable and end up rock hard. Fabric choices will affect the softness to a degree.

If you use a tougher fabric than the sofa originally had, it will be a little harder to sit on. However, the choice of stuffing will really make the difference. Do not let someone talk you into something you haven't tried sitting on. If they do not have the kind of cushion you want, go elsewhere.

2. **Check out the workshop.** You would be amazed at some of the places I have seen. Be sure the reupholsterer does not smoke in the shop. There is nothing worse than spending a fortune on a sofa only to have it stink of stale cigarette smoke! And believe it or not, it happens a lot.

3. **Ask for references and follow up on them.** Find out how long it took for the work to get done. Was the estimate accurate? Was the customer completely satisfied?

4. **Check out at least three different upholsterers.** Have each one estimate the yardage and the labor. Discuss replacement cushions in advance. Know what options each upholsterer offers and uses for its estimate.

5. **Most upholsterers expect you to purchase the fabric from them.** If you do not, they will usually charge you a higher fee for labor, since they will not be making any profit on fabric purchased elsewhere. From my experience, you will usually find a larger selection of fabrics at a furniture store, design studio, or fabric store. So select your fabric sample before getting the final estimate. It will make a difference.

6. **Ask questions.** Find out if the estimate includes retying the springs. Does it include arm covers or arm caps? Will the deck (the part of the sofa under the cushions) be covered in matching fabric or in muslin? Will the cushions be reversible? In other words, will they match on both sides so they can be flipped over? How long is the work guaranteed for? What exactly is covered in the guarantee?

7. **Be sure when comparing estimates that you are comparing apples to apples.** Then follow your instincts. Always hire the person you feel most comfortable with. Do not make your decision based just on price. Of course, don't be afraid to discuss lower estimates you have received for the same work. I think it is helpful for people to know what the competition is charging. An honest reupholsterer should be able to give you a reason-

able explanation for the difference in price. I, personally, would be very wary of someone who bad-mouthed the competition. This is usually not a good sign. It's one thing to be able to cite actual examples, but another to freely gossip.

By now you must realize that by the time all is said and done, you basically have a new sofa!

This should explain why reupholstering is often as expensive as or even more expensive than buying a new sofa! So be sure that this is really the one you want to live with for a long time.

Don't believe the foolish idea that just because it's old, it's better quality. Honestly, even old stuff can be cheap stuff. And you still get what you pay for!

Slipcovering

I am thrilled to see the rebirth of the slipcover. For many years, it was almost impossible to find anyone who was capable of making a slipcover. Fortunately, it has made a remarkable comeback over the past few years. Now even furniture manufacturers are getting into the act. Many of them now make available a slipcover that can be ordered at the time you purchase your furniture.

So what is a slipcover? Well, it is pretty much what it sounds like—a cover that you slip over your furniture.

There are a variety of styles. Currently, the trend seems to be an unfinished look, like a sheet or throw with a few tucks here and there. Actually, I would prefer to term this style a *throw,* as opposed to a slipcover.

THROWS

Throws are actually less expensive to produce. First of all, you do not have to "fit" the throw to the cushions. Instead, as the name implies, it is usually a large, one-piece unit that is literally thrown over the furniture. All of the shaping is the result of tucks, pleats, or gathers in strategic places. This style works best on large, overstuffed furniture.

I recommend having a throw lined, especially if you have a patterned or darker color sofa. The lining will keep sofa fabric from showing through. When ordering a throw, check the cleaning recommendations. You would most definitely want to be able to clean it easily. Usually dry cleaning is recommended, even if the label says "washable." Washing almost any upholstery fabric will remove any sizing or body. However, some fabrics cannot be dry-cleaned. They may even melt if dry-cleaned. So be very careful when selecting fabric. After all, what is the point in having a throw if it can't be cleaned?

The throw works extremely well if you happen to have a wonderful old sofa that fits your taste just perfectly, but whose fabric has seen better days. Throws are relatively inexpensive, because they are not very labor intensive. Most of the cost is in the fabric.

Throws also work well in protecting a new or good sofa from being destroyed by normal everyday living. If you have children, pets, or even a messy spouse and you are purchasing new furniture, you may want to consider ordering a throw at the same time. It could greatly extend the life of your sofa.

SLIPCOVERS

Slipcovers, as opposed to throws, are actually fitted or tailored to the exact shape of the furniture.

This is where the ability of the seamstress really comes into play. And finding a really good slipcover seamstress can be difficult. As I said earlier in this chapter, it was nearly a dead trade.

My slipcover seamstress is in her late seventies and we have been trying for years to find a younger person she could teach the trade to—with no luck! Anyway, you definitely want to take a look at work a seamstress has previously done. Try and check out more than one job. It's important. Why? Well, because this kind of work requires the same kind of ability and skill that a tailor needs to make a suit.

Slipcovers generally have a piece that covers the basic frame section of the sofa. If you remove all the cushions, what's left is the part that the first section is fitted to. This section also has a skirt attached to it. And just like with reupholstering, you can change the style of the skirt to a degree. Obviously, if the sofa originally had a shirred or gath-

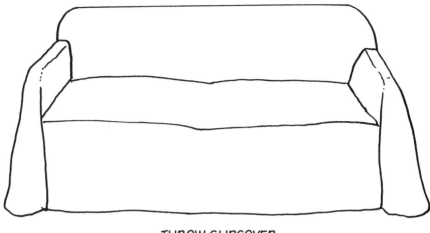

THROW SLIPCOVER

ered skirt, it is going to be very difficult to camouflage that with a straight skirt.

If your original sofa is tufted (it looks as though you took your fingers and pushed the fabric in at even intervals, creating indentations), expect that it will be difficult to get a good fit over the tufting. On occasions, I have used a poly matting cover to help fill in the gaps. If your seamstress is really good, this can work. If your sofa has attached or semiattached back cushions, it will require perfect fitting to get a really good look. Using *cording* between the cushion lines usually helps. Cording is a decorative trim made from several stringlike strands that are twisted together to create a rope. *Welts* are basically the same thing, but are usually made out of string that is covered by fabric—most often, the same fabric you are using to make the slipcover, but you also can choose a contrasting colored fabric.

Next, the individual cushions are fitted with new covers. Sometimes, depending on the original fabric and style of the cushions, you may want to remove the original cushion covers, particularly if the original cushions had welts or cording on them. They really can be a problem to keep straight under a new cover. Again, you have an opportunity to change the style of seaming. Seaming can be done with a welt or cord. It can also be weltless, or you can even have a contrasting cord added.

Most slipcover seamstresses will work only in cotton-weight fabric. Chintzes (highly polished or glazed fabrics), printed cotton, linen, corduroy, lightweight velvet, and denim are usually acceptable. But most seamstresses will not work in upholstery or heavier-weight fabrics. I have convinced my seamstress on occasion to use a heavier-weight fabric, but only if it does not have a coating on the back side. Often, a binding-type liquid is applied to the back of the fabric to give it more stability. This makes the fabric much stiffer and very difficult to work with.

Okay, you've chosen a fabric. What next? The seamstress should come to your home to measure and fit the sofa. One of the nice things about slipcovers is that the sofa never has to leave your home. Once the fitting has been done, the seamstress will do most of the sewing at the shop. Once the majority of that is finished, the seamstress will come back to apply and finish the slipcover at your home. And voila—your sofa will look almost new! Why did I say "almost" new? Well, you have to be realistic. If your existing cushions are mashed and mat-

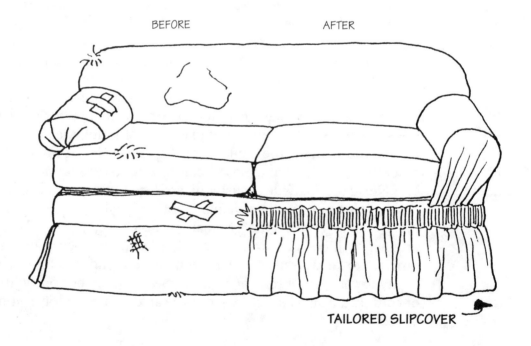

BEFORE   AFTER

TAILORED SLIPCOVER

ted, they will still be mashed and matted. But if you've chosen a great seamstress, the fit should be nearly as good as the original upholstery fit was.

Of course, some pieces of furniture lend themselves better to slipcovers than others. No matter how good a seamstress is, making a slipcover fit a curved tub chair (a chair that is shaped almost like half of a barrel) is nearly impossible!

The yardage requirements for slipcovers will be about the same as for reupholstering, and sometimes even a little more. But the labor costs are much less than upholstery work. That is one of the big advantages of doing slipcovers. Another advantage is that if your existing fabric is still in great shape, you now have the option of changing the look without spending a fortune.

Again, be smart. Check out estimates from several different people before signing on the dotted line. Where do you find a slipcover seamstress? Check with design studios, fabric stores, furniture stores, drapery shops, and of course, the yellow pages.

A word of caution—just like with the throw, try out a test sample before proceeding. You want to be sure that the sofa's original fabric does not show through your new fabric. So it is definitely worth buying a sample and trying it out.

Don't forget to ask if there is a different price structure if you don't purchase your fabric from the seamstress. And while you're at it, don't be afraid to compare prices on fabric. Usually the same fabric will be available from several sources. If you are buying your fabric from a discount outlet, be sure that the fabric is in one continuous piece. Sometimes, an outlet will sell you the correct amount of yardage in two separate pieces. This is okay if the individual piece sizes are large enough to cut the patterns or pieces you need for each section of the sofa. So be sure to check with your seamstress before agreeing to purchase fabric that is not in one continuous piece. Find out what size "cuts" (pieces) the seamstress needs to get the pattern to fit. You may have to purchase an extra yard to get the right cuts.

Be aware of the pattern repeats on your fabric. This too, can affect the amount of yardage required. For example, a floral pattern with a repeat of 36 inches can add as much as 45 percent more fabric to an estimate! This is especially true if you want the floral pattern placed in the center of each seat and back cushion.

Ultimately, slipcovers work best on straight-lined pieces of furniture with loose seat and back cushions. They give the best fit.

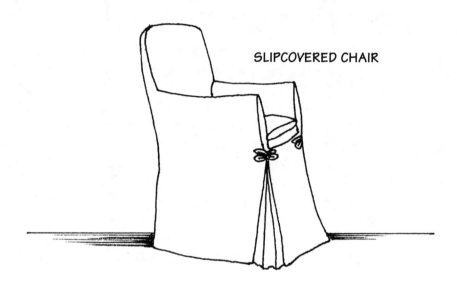

SLIPCOVERED CHAIR

Shopping Notes

When deciding whether or not to invest money in an existing piece of upholstered furniture, first compare the costs of buying new. If your goal is just to buy a few more years of use, then consider buying an inexpensive new piece instead.

If you are absolutely in love with your existing furniture and expect to keep it for the next seven years, then go ahead and reupholster.

Choose a slipcover if you are just looking for a simple change in fabric, to make seasonal changes.

The bottom line: always, always get at least three estimates.

Words of Wisdom

Always look at fabric selections in the same kind of light that you have at home.

Fluorescent lights change the color of fabric.

Try the samples in natural light and incandescent (regular light bulbs).

Never, ever, look at fabric with rose-colored glasses (or any other color-tinted glasses)! The world may look better with them on, but it is very difficult to match colors that way.

4

WHAT ARE CASE GOODS AND WHY DOES ONE PIECE COST $250 AND THE OTHER $2,500?

ase goods can be defined as any piece of furniture that has a basic "case" or box design and is used for storage or display. Wardrobes, dressers, bureaus, and cabinets all belong in this category. In the home fashions industry, bedroom and dining room collections (or sets) are also lumped into the category of case goods, as are wall systems and any freestanding cabinetry.

Of course, as in most "cases" in life, there are exceptions to the rule. And the exception with regard to case goods is tables. For the most part, tables are classified as *occasional furniture*. This category includes end tables, cocktail tables, wine tables, book tables, and other ornamental pieces. However, dining tables will always be found with the case goods. The reason for this, I suppose, is that dining room tables are often included in dining room collections, or there might be a matching traditional case good, such as a buffet, server, or china cabinet, that comes with the dining table.

Case goods and occasional furniture do not necessarily have to be made of wood. Marble, glass, laminate, and plastic are just some of the materials used in these two furniture groups. The basic defining difference is that they are not upholstered.

A few quick thoughts when it comes to choosing occasional furniture: I think that a cocktail table in particular should have a character of its own. This is an opportunity to really express yourself. Have fun with this piece of furniture. Sofas, chairs, and even dining tables have to be comfortable or practical. The cocktail table is not necessarily required to have such standards. After all, you usually don't sit on it! But you may put your feet on it, you may eat on it, you may play games and you may dance on it! So, have fun with it. Get creative. Allow yourself to go wild!

Here are some of the basic types of case goods available.

Armoires or Wardrobes

This is one of my favorite pieces of furniture. I suppose that if I could only afford one piece, it would be an armoire.

Today, armoires are used in almost every room of the home. They are very adaptable. When purchasing an armoire, try to determine all the different ways you may want to use it over a lifetime of ownership. That way, you can select a style that is flexible and also be sure that the interior measurements will accommodate many different uses.

Armoires are an ideal piece of furniture for apartments. They can double as a TV/stereo wall system and as storage for sweaters, blankets, pillows, or other bulky things. They can be used as a china cabinet. And they can be used for a variety of storage needs in the bedroom.

One of the problems frequently encountered with many armoires is that the depth (the dimension from front to back) is not enough to house a television or computer. So if your intention is to use one for a television or computer, you may have to make some adjustments. But don't fret—there is almost always a way to make it work. You can remove the back if necessary. If you need to gain only a few inches, you can accomplish this simply by pulling the armoire a few inches away from the wall and either cutting a hole in the back or removing it entirely.

Many styles today can be outfitted with different interiors when you order them. Again, be sure to check the inside measurements to make sure they fit your specific needs. Just because the manufacturer says an

Armoires were originally designed to be closets. They actually fit together like a puzzle, so you could take them apart and transport them easily. Some of the European armoires are still made this way. I have one from West Germany that breaks down into three pieces.

ARMOIRE

armoire is designed for use with a TV or computer doesn't mean *your* computer will fit!

A big consideration when purchasing such a large piece of furniture is whether you will actually be able to get it to the spot you had planned for it. Turning corners with an enormous, unyielding cabinet like this can be virtually impossible. And, unfortunately, most of the armoires produced today are all in one piece. I have had to remove stair railings and door trims to deliver an armoire. On one occasion, I had to remove a window and use a drywall elevator truck to bring an armoire into a bedroom through the window!

Dressers and Chests

Dressers and chests are two of the most commonly purchased items for a bedroom. Historically, the woman will use the dresser and the man will use the chest, unless it is a lingerie chest. But it really is a matter of preference and space.

CHEST-ON-CHEST

Most collections offer at least two different choices for dressers. One will usually be smaller in width, with drawers. The other is longer—a triple dresser—and has a combination of drawers and doors. There are usually drawers behind the doors, which means that every time you need something, you will need to open two things—the door and the drawer. I don't recommend this without first having your coffee in the morning!

Chests also offer a few different choices: *chest-on-chest*—wider drawers on the bottom and narrower drawers on top; *chest of drawers*—a smaller chest with just drawers; and a third style with doors on top. In this case, the doors on top do not have drawers behind them—go figure! Anyway, choosing the style is really a matter of personal choice and the amount of space you have to work with.

I prefer to have a large, well-organized closet rather than a dresser or chest. But that is just my style. I have an armoire in the bedroom, which houses my television along with all of the other things I can't figure out where else to put.

Most collections include both the dining and the bedroom furniture. They are usually produced in the same plant, making the production setup more efficient and cost-effective.

On occasion, you may find that something that was designed for the bedroom, for example, will actually work better in your dining room. I have used a dresser as a buffet effectively.

Sizes will vary from one collection to the next, so repeat after me—measure, and measure again.

Beds

Beds are available in three basic sizes: twin—3/3 (which means 3 feet 3 inches), queen—5/0 (five feet 0 inches), and king—6/6 (six feet six inches). If you are buying a new bed, be aware that most manufac-

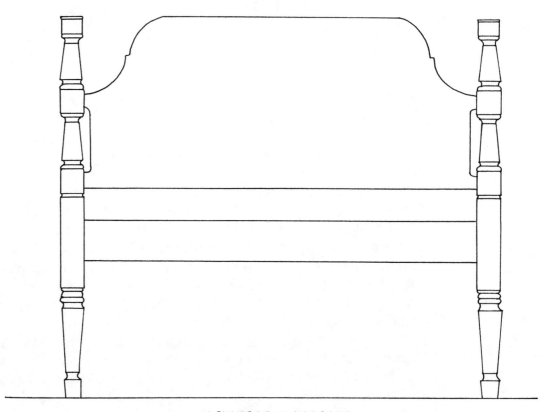

LOW POST HEADBOARD

FOOTBOARD

turers no longer make full size, since there is so little difference between queen and full. Instead, they drill two sets of hardware holes into the queen-size bed to accommodate both sizes. Full size is 54 inches wide by 75 inches long, queen size is 60 inches wide by 80 inches long, and king size is 72 inches wide by 80 inches long. Twin size is 39 inches wide by 75 inches long.

A standard bed consists of just a headboard. You usually need to purchase a metal bed frame separately, which can then be attached to the headboard.

Some beds have a footboard available as an option. If you purchase a bed with both a headboard and footboard, then the metal sides (frame) are supplied.

A *tester bed* is one with tall spindles at the headboard and/or footboard.

A *canopy bed* is a tester bed with an optional canopy frame. The canopy frame is attached to the tall spindles of the foot- and headboards.

A *storage headboard* is exactly what it sounds like—a headboard with storage. Sometimes this is a padded or upholstered headboard, sometimes not.

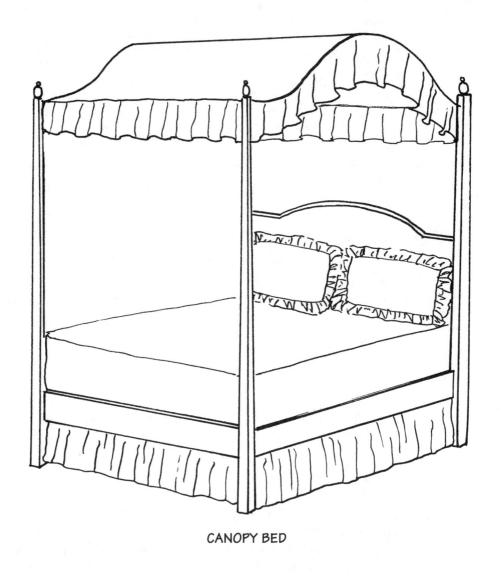

CANOPY BED

A *daybed* consists of three sides. The headboard and footboard are the same height and a sideboard fits between them on one side. This side now becomes the back. A daybed can be used as a sofa in the day and a bed at night, hence the name.

Another option for a headboard is an *upholstered headboard*. There are manufacturers that specialize in this product. A variety of styles and shapes are available.

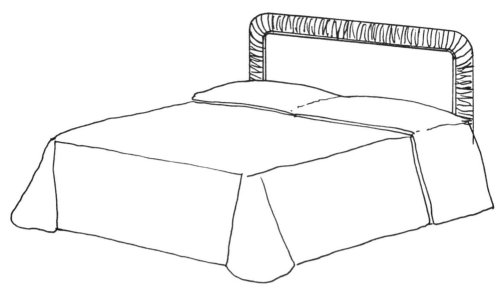

UPHOLSTERED HEADBOARD

Buffets and China Cabinets

Most china cabinets are produced in two pieces—the base, which can double as a buffet, and the top, which is the hutch, or display unit. This makes sense in a lot of ways. Obviously, moving a 72-inch wide by 84-inch tall piece of furniture would be next to impossible. Secondly, being made of two parts gives the piece more flexibility in its use. A smaller china cabinet, no larger than 54 inches in width, is produced in one piece, but this size is difficult to find.

Some china hutches have a lighted interior. There are basically two different ways to light the inside. The less expensive method is to use elongated incandescent light bulbs, which are positioned behind a wood strip. The second and more expensive method is to use recessed lighting in the top of the unit. Some use parabolic or reflector bulbs and others use halogen bulbs. Halogen bulbs are smaller, more expensive, and get much hotter, but produce a whiter light and take up less room. The shelves inside a hutch are usually glass to allow the light to filter down through them. If you are planning on displaying plates in an upright position, check to be sure that the glass has a groove cut into it.

Some collections offer full-length display cabinets. They are generally narrower, about 36 to 42 inches wide. They are wonderful if used as pairs. They can be used in both the dining and living room, to display a variety of items. Sometimes they will be lit, both from the top and the bottom.

Most dining collections offer a serving cabinet. The top of the server will usually open up to expose a heat-proof surface from which to serve a buffet. It may have storage beneath or, in some cases, be open for display.

Wall Systems

Because of the flexibility and practicality of wall systems, they are very popular in both the bedroom and the dining room. Wall systems provide a great amount of storage in a minimum of space. They are available in both traditional and contemporary styles. A wall system usually consists of *pier cabinets, light bridges, storage headboards, dressers* or *buffets,* and *mirrors.* These can be put together to create an entire wall of furniture. Pier cabinets are tall, narrow (around 20 to 24 inches wide) cabinets that usually have drawers on the bottom and doors on the top. They are usually around 82 to 84 inches tall. A light bridge is much like a valance—a piece of wood 60 to 80 inches wide by 8 to 12 inches high. It often has lights inside. The light bridge is attached between two pier cabinets. Then you can put either a bed, a dresser, or a buffet under the light bridge. Mirrors can be added to fill in the open wall space from the top of the bed to the bottom of the light bridge.

Dining Tables

Some tables come with a *leaf,* or extension. Some do not. The number of leaves that a table can hold will have an effect on the price. Some leaves have an *apron* (matching the side edge of the table), others do not. Instead, there will be a gap on the side of the table when the leaves are inserted. This will also change the price. How stable a table is with the leaves in place is very important. Always try a table with

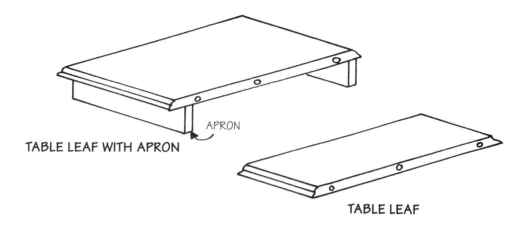

TABLE LEAF WITH APRON

APRON

TABLE LEAF

the leaves in before buying it. Make sure the hardware used to support the leaves is of good, durable quality. Does it lock in place? Does the table open easily? Or will it require the high school football team to open? If the table has a pedestal base, does it split in two when you open the top to insert the leaves?

There are basically two different heights of tables. Dining tables are about 28 inches high. Game tables, which are 24 to 26 inches high, can be used as dining tables, but you must be sure to purchase chairs that are the corresponding height! Otherwise, you could end up with your chin resting on your knees! If you are mixing different styles, you must be very careful in this area.

Two questions often asked about dining tables are, How much room do I need for each person or place setting at a table? and How much room do I need to comfortably pull a chair out for sitting?

The basic answer to the first question is that you will need approximately 18 inches per place setting. However, you will need more than 18 inches for each chair! How much room you will need for each chair depends on which chair you purchase. So just because someone says a dining table will accommodate eight people, it does not necessarily mean it will accommodate eight of your chairs.

The kind of table you have also affects the number of people you can seat. If the legs of your tables are large, they will be in the way of anyone sitting too near the corners. If your table has extra legs, used to accommodate large extension tables, then you will not be able to seat anyone where you have extra legs.

The answer to the second question is a little bit simpler. You will need a minimum of 30 inches of space, from the edge of the table, to allow for comfortable seating. Obviously, if you are seating larger people or using larger chairs, you will need more room. I try to allow 36 inches from the edge of the table for each chair when planning a room. So if the dining table is 38 inches wide, you will need to add 72 inches to this measurement to allow for a chair on either side to make sure you have enough room from the wall (a total of 110 inches). Which means you had better have a room that is about 9 feet 6 inches wide.

Sometimes it makes more sense to choose a round table. If your room is a perfect square, this can make it look much more open and spacious. If you are wedded to your square table, you may want to turn it on an angle (rather than have the edges of the table parallel to the walls) to create the optical illusion of more space. I have a 54-inch round table around which I have placed four large chairs, with their backs facing the corners of the room. It is a great look. When entertaining more than four people, my table accommodates up to three extension leaves. I then use a combination of two different styles of chairs. It creates a very elegant atmosphere and fools the eye into believing there is more space than actually exists.

Dining Chairs

Dining chairs are also considered case goods. Chairs really vary a lot in price. Sometimes price has to do with quality, but not always. Many chairs are not manufactured in America, but imported. When a new style is first introduced, it is usually fairly expensive. But soon, a myriad of suppliers start to copy the original design. And, as in other industries, this drives the price down. If a style does not get copied, then of course the price will remain high. Dining chairs can cost as little as $99 and as much as $600 apiece.

Arm chairs are always more expensive than armless. The joints of a chair should be glued, screwed, or doweled. It is preferable for the back of the chair to be one continuous piece down through the leg. This is the most durable construction. Having a break at the seat will make for a weak chair. Added struts or slats between the legs of the chair will obviously make it stronger.

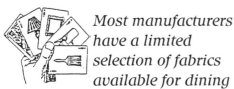 *Most manufacturers have a limited selection of fabrics available for dining chairs. If you cannot find something you like from this selection, you may want to choose a basic fabric and then have a custom fabric applied later.*

There are basically two styles of chair seat cushions. The first is called a *slip seat*. This is a flat cushion without cording or trim. The fabric is simply folded over the frame and stapled on the underside. It is very easy to redo a slip seat, so changing fabric is not a big deal.

The second style is called a *box seat*. Much as it sounds, it is shaped like a box. It may or may not have cording or trim at the seam between the top and side of the seat. Changing fabric on this style is more difficult because it requires sewing.

Many dining room chairs have cane or rattan backs. This is a great look and is popular on many different styles. Just a few words of caution: fine-knit clothing will catch on this material. If you have guests with expensive knit clothing, it is wise to provide a cloth or slipcover for their chair. If you are a cat owner, beware—your pet will find a cane or rattan back an irresistible scratching post!

Barstools

Never, ever, buy a barstool or counter stool that does not have an extra support between the legs. Without extra support, the length of the leg is too long to brace the weight a stool must bear.

Barstools and counter stools often are available to match dining chairs. With today's open living plans, the kitchen and/or dining areas often have an island or bar. However, do not use the overall height dimension in determining your selection, because it also includes the height of the back as part of the measurement. Be sure to use only the actual *seat height* for determining the correct choice. And it is always nice if the barstool or counter stool has a metal rail instead of a wood rail to rest your feet on. Metal will clean and hold up much better.

Construction—Wood and Other Materials

SOLID VERSUS VENEER

I guess the next thing to do is to clear up some misconceptions about case goods and wood furniture. Unfortunately, most of us were indoctrinated by our parents or grandparents in regard to wood furniture construction. We have the idea that unless something is *solid* wood, as opposed to veneering or chip core, then it must be poor quality.

Well, nothing could be further from the truth!

The old veneer process was defective. And as a result, it did peel, chip, ripple, and shift. However, the basic idea of veneering is a sound one. Why? Well, veneering is actually a solution to a big problem with solid wood furniture: warping! Wood absorbs moisture, even if it is kiln dried and kept in an air-conditioned home. As a result, it warps in the direction of the grain. But if you have layer upon layer of veneering,

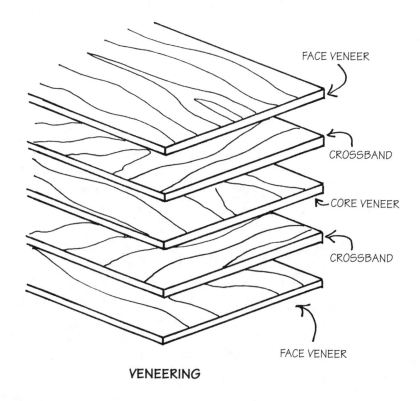

FACE VENEER

CROSSBAND

CORE VENEER

CROSSBAND

FACE VENEER

VENEERING

then the grain actually runs in different directions, making it impossible for the wood to warp. One layer keeps the next layer in line. With today's technology, veneering is durable and beautiful. Actually, some of the eighteenth-century designs incorporated a lot of veneer work. And we certainly consider that furniture to have quality.

Another advantage of veneering is that it allows the most beautiful parts of the wood to be used in the most decorative manner, such as on the top of a dining table. Imagine being able to create a starburst effect on the top of a round dining table. Isn't that preferable to the grain just running straight across? Of course it is. You can also create beautiful banding effects, such as a border on the top of a table. This would not be possible with solid wood surfaces.

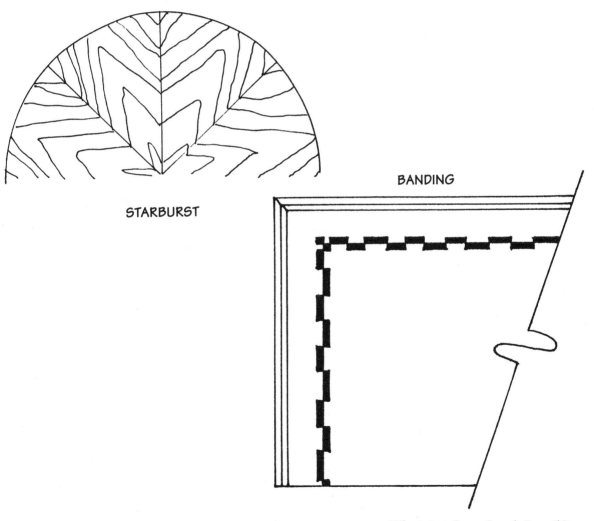

STARBURST

BANDING

Okay, so what is under the veneer? Who cares! I'm only half kidding here. The fact is that it really is not that important. A customer once asked what kind of wood was under the Formica finish of her table. Although I did respond with "Who cares!" I really meant, was she planning on removing the Formica? The same is true with veneer. But to answer the question, veneer is usually applied over chip core or solid wood.

Yes, I said *chip core*. It's a bad word to a lot of people. Actually, chip core is an excellent product. Because chip core consists of small pieces of wood bonded together, their grains run in all sorts of directions. So you will not have a problem with moisture absorption or warping. It is a very solid construction. Besides, it is also a green product. You know, conserve the forests, use every piece of wood scrap before you cut down another tree. Who isn't in favor of that? And yes, there are different qualities of chip core. Naturally, the more expensive a piece of furniture, the better quality chip core that will be used.

If the term *solids* or *solid wood* is used today, it may mean that the furniture is entirely made from wood, as opposed to plastic. For the most part, solid wood furniture is made from a combination of solid, chip, and veneer woods. It is very rare to find a piece of furniture made completely of solid wood, without some veneering. The few exceptions are pine, oak, and sometimes maple. And with these woods, there will be some inherent problems that can occur because it is solid. A solid pine or oak table will experience cracking over time, particularly at the knots of the wood. This can be repaired by adding a filler into the cracks and then sanding and sealing the finish.

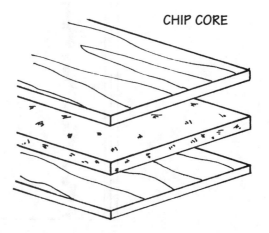

CHIP CORE

Another misconception: oak is the only species of wood that is considered *hardwood*. A lot of different species are classified as hardwoods, like walnut, maple, cherry, and mahogany. And with today's technologies, almost any wood can be given a hard finish. I'll discuss this later, under Finishing.

Here's the biggest shock to buyers of solid wood furniture: even some of the most expensive pieces of wood furniture have a plywood back. Relax, it's okay. Unless, of course, you were planning on putting this piece of furniture in the middle of the room with it's back showing! In that case, you will probably have to get a cabinetmaker to make you a new back to match the rest of the piece. The manufacturer will not do this.

Okay, so why does one piece cost $250 and another $2,500? Well, I've explained a few of the differences so far. But there is still a lot more to explore. Technology has allowed us to do some interesting things. For example, it is possible to photograph or duplicate the pattern or grain of wood and reproduce it on laminates (plastic) or even heavy-duty cardboard. So now, instead of using the expensive, pretty-grained part of wood for veneering, we can use this inexpensive "forgery." Often, when you see an ad for "three rooms of furniture for just $395.00," this is the kind of furniture you are getting!

Now, don't get me wrong. Plastic laminates such as Formica brand are terrific, and I use them often. They are the perfect choice for many applications. I just want you to be aware of what you are getting for your money. Just because it *looks* like wood, does not mean that it *is* wood.

Here are some more tips on elements that affect the cost of wood furniture. Whether or not the wood has been kiln dried will make a difference in how it will react to climate changes. Kiln-dried wood is also more expensive. The species of wood will also drastically affect the cost. Obviously some woods are more readily available than others. And the more different types of wood used in any given piece, the more expensive that piece will be.

How a piece is joined together will certainly affect its durability and life. A stapled joint in a drawer will never outlast a well-glued and doweled one. Most manufacturers of fine furniture use glued, screwed, and corner-blocked construction for the basic case.

The style or design will also greatly affect the price. If a piece has carving or complex details that require more hands-on work, then it will obviously cost more. The more intricate the veneer patterning, the more expensive.

Speaking of carving, often the term *hand-carved* is used in reference to the details of the wood. What does this mean? Well, actually it is a very interesting process. First, a craftsman designs and carves the original piece. Then his pattern is duplicated. At the manufacturing plant, several computerized carving machines are set up. Then a mechanic-craftsman begins the carving and all the other machines follow. Therefore, a real person is actually controlling the carving of several pieces at once. Hence, the term *hand-carved*.

Of course, if you want a designer-label brand, you will pay more, just as with clothing! The bigger the name, the more expensive. It has nothing to do with quality, but everything to do with style.

Options

As always, if there are options, the price will go up. So what kinds of options are available? Well, unlike upholstered furniture, there's not a lot to choose from. But you can select various finishes. And sometimes, you will have a choice of sizes. Occasionally, you will be able to add or change hardware, pulls, or casters and wheels. Yes, wheels! Even some eighteenth-century styles had little wheel casters.

DRAWERS

Let's talk drawers! Furniture people love to talk about *dovetailing*. No, it isn't really a dove's tail, but it is shaped like one—sort of. Dovetailing is a form of construction used to join two pieces of wood together. The pieces are notched with wedge-shaped projections that fit together to create a joint. This technique is usually reserved for the construction of drawers. But occasionally, for the visual effect, it will be used on the corners of a piece. The wood will expand as it absorbs moisture in the summer (and the pieces will fit closer together), and it will contract again in the winter as it loses moisture. On less expensive furniture, staples, glue, or other metal fasteners are used. Obviously, they won't help much if the two pieces of wood decide to go their separate ways!

Another feature on a drawer is the *glide*. This is the apparatus that allows the drawer to slide open and keeps it straight as it does. There are basically two types of glides—metal and wood. People have differing opinions about which is better. Wood glides can sometimes stick or bind, but they are still considered to be preferable. By their very nature, metal glides don't stick or bind, but they have received a bad reputation from furniture purists who still believe the old-fashioned way is the only way. As in all things, there are different qualities of product available. I think that a well-designed, good-quality metal glide can be terrific. If you are a purist, you will probably insist on a wood glide. However, in the end, this is not usually something you have a choice on—manufacturers do not offer options on this feature. Basically, if you want a certain piece of furniture, you will get whatever kind of glide the manufacturer has chosen to use.

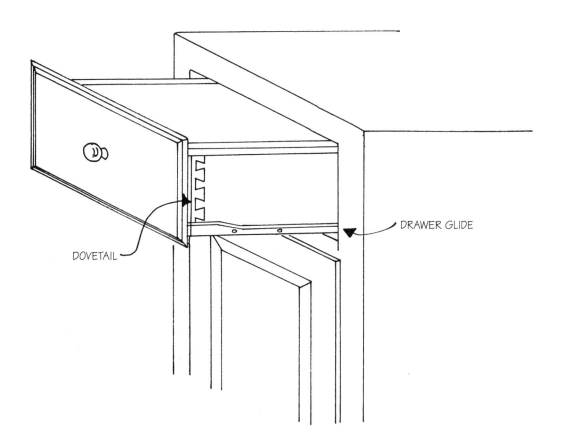

DOVETAIL

DRAWER GLIDE

HARDWARE

Hardware, or "pulls," are attached to the exterior of the door or drawer and are used for pulling them open. The basic difference is whether they are solid or plated, in white metal or brass. And there are different qualities of plating. An inexpensive plated piece of hardware will lose its plating within a year. The more decorative the hardware, the more expensive. And, of course, the greater the number of pieces of hardware, the more expensive.

FINISHES

Most American-manufactured case goods are only available in the finish shown. Occasionally, you will have a choice of two or three different finishes.

However, many manufacturers are now importing many of their wood pieces. And most of these are shipped into this country unfinished. So a whole new world has literally opened up. There are many manufacturers now set up to supply these pieces in a variety of finishes. This is where it really gets fun! I love playing with different finishes—it is amazing how different a chair can look when you change its color or use an antique finish versus a high-gloss finish.

Speaking of finishes—this is definitely one of the areas that has the biggest effect on the price! This is what defines "quality" versus just furniture.

Finishing is an art. It takes hours of sanding, washing, staining, highlighting, sealing, baking, rubbing with steel wool, and hand waxing to get a really good quality finish. Then you have different styles of finishing. An antique look requires a good craftsman to "wear out" the finish in just the right places. Another technique uses a "splattering" effect. The finish is literally splattered with a dark-colored stain to give it a ruggedly aged look.

A little trick that I use is to ask if an unfinished piece is available, and then have a custom finish applied by a cabinetmaker. Many of the manufacturers will accommodate this, and occasionally, you can get them to give you a 10 or 15 percent discount. In the end, it will cost more to do this, but it can be worth it if it is exactly what you want.

Then you have all of the different kinds of coatings that can be applied. Often, I have used an "impervious" finish on a table that will be getting a lot of use and abuse by a family. My cabinetmaker uses catalyzed lacquer to create this miracle finish. But you must make sure that it is compatible with whatever the manufacturer has already used. If not, you may end up with a sticky mess when a chemical reaction takes place.

Another way to make a tabletop "family-proof" is to have glass cut to fit it. Glass may show fingerprints, but you can clean it with a little Windex. And that is a whole lot easier than trying to remove rings, scratches, and dents from the top of the table!

On occasion, manufacturers will make different materials available for the top of the table, such as plastic laminates, marble, and glass. All of these can change the look and the price.

Making the Right Choice

Over the years, I have found that most people replace their upholstery items every seven to ten years. But case goods tend to hang around a lot longer. So do take your time in selecting them. You will probably be looking at that dining room set for fifteen to twenty years minimum!

Use the Ink Blot theory with furniture. Find your own style. The best advice I can give you is take the time to window-shop and browse. I recommend spending at least a month looking in furniture stores and design showrooms, and don't forget antique shops and collectible galleries. Take time going through design magazines and catalogs to educate yourself on all the options you really have. Cut out or take notes on the kind of style that keeps attracting you. But be careful when analyzing photos of rooms. Try to decipher whether it is the furniture you like or the room itself. Maybe it's just the wallpaper or accessories that grab you. Learn to be specific about exactly what attracts you to a space. If, for example, every photo you collect seems to have different styles of furniture, but each one shows a rich forest green color scheme with plaid fabric, then obviously you have found your overall style, but not necessarily the style of your furniture.

Be aware of the proportions of your living space. Men seem to like larger, darker furniture. That's great, as long as the room the furniture is going into can accommodate it. Years ago, a bed style known as Paul Bunyan was very popular. It was an enormous bed, much like a tree—hence the name. Anyway, it amazed me how many people were willing to cram this monster of a bed into tiny bungalow rooms!

If you have any doubt about whether or not something will actually fit into a room or through a door or hall, let the salesperson know up front. She may want to come to your home to see for herself or send a delivery person in advance of your purchase.

If you are contemplating new flooring or carpeting along with a new dining or bedroom set, please arrange to do the floor first! Carpet and flooring installers will not empty your china cabinet or armoire. Nor are they expected to move furniture.

Shopping Notes

Never walk into a store and ask to see a "suite" of furniture. This is a passé term that indicates you have not been shopping for furniture in eons! Yes, manufacturers do make suites, but they are called *collections*. Collections are much more interesting. You see, things do not have to match! That's very boring, and it limits your flexibility in decorating now and in the future.

Today's collections allow you much more freedom and choice. After all, isn't that what we all want? Just because the furniture is pictured one way in the catalog does not mean that is the only way it can be used.

If you are not comfortable mixing things up, then go ahead and find a collection that makes you happy. Most of the collections today are by designers, so you really cannot go wrong.

What if you can afford to buy only one or two pieces now and you want to buy more from the same collection in the future? First find out how long the collection has been available. If something has been around for four or five years already, I would be concerned about how much longer it will be available.

Manufacturers only have so much capacity for production. If they decide to add a new style to their lineup, then something must be discontinued. And **manufacturers can discontinue without notice!** The sales representatives for the manufacturers usually have some idea of

One of the latest style trends is a unique combination of old and new. Old architectural pieces such as doors, gates, windows, moldings, and pediments from old homes or antique furniture are being used to create new furniture. An antique door may be used as the basis of a wall system or a new china cabinet. An old iron gate can be made into the top of a table and then covered with glass. These pieces look wonderful and are a pleasure to create.

what is going on. It is advisable that you ask your salesperson to check with the sales representative to see if he is aware of any discontinuation plans.

Sometimes, a manufacturer will discontinue a style only to change its color and name. I am amazed to find the same piece of furniture twelve months later with a brand new number and name. Often the manufacturer hasn't even changed the color. Instead, it will take a piece from one collection and move it to another.

When ordering furniture, expect to wait six to twelve weeks for anything that is not in stock at the store. Case goods collections are usually produced two to four times a year. This is called a *cutting*. And if you have just missed a cutting, then you could be waiting as long as six months!

Only the largest stores will have something in stock. Most will not sell the floor sample—they need it to show other customers and they cannot afford to be without a sample for weeks or months.

It is common procedure for stores to sell from catalogs. You may not like this idea, but it is an industry standard. They use the samples they have in the store as an example of the manufacturers' quality. If you feel you must see every piece before you purchase, be prepared to drive all over Timbuktu to accomplish this.

It is helpful if your salesperson or designer has actually sat in any dining chair you are considering. This is the biggest drawback of purchasing from catalogs. Some chairs are comfortable and some are horrible. However, often the buyer or someone within the store may have seen the piece you are considering.

And yes, you are also expected to select stain colors from a page in the catalog. Some manufacturers may have small wood samples available, but many do not. How close will the actual color be to the sample? Close enough to meet their quality control standards. Do remember, even wood will look different under various kinds of lighting.

Choose a color keeping in mind the kind of lighting you expect to use with the furniture.

All furniture that you order is considered "custom ordered." It is not returnable.

Damage can, and usually does, happen in shipping. Few pieces of wood furniture make it to the retailer without at least a scratch or two. This is expected. However, you are not expected to accept it "as is." The retailer should have a "furniture doctor" to fix all nicks, scratches, or other damage. The retailer may choose to do this in your home after delivery. It all depends on the retailer. Some customers will withhold a small portion of the final payment until this is done. (For your information, a small portion is defined as 10 percent, not 50 percent!)

Sometimes the damage from shipping is significant. Realize that most retailers are used to dealing with these situations. The standard procedure is to work with the manufacturer and do most repairs on site. If something is beyond repair, then it will need to be replaced. Things like this do happen, so don't take it personally. If you had ordered your furniture for a really special occasion, it is possible for the retailer to lend you something until your furniture can be delivered. If the salesperson is not sure about delivery expectations, have her call the manufacturer and check the availability. If you expect to have your dining room set for Thanksgiving, be sure it will actually be available before then.

You will be required to put a deposit down for anything you order. Twenty percent is pretty much the standard. Read the sales agreement before you sign it, including the fine print.

Find out if the retailer charges for delivery: some do and some don't. You may be charged by the piece or by the distance. Find out all charges that may apply. Most retailers do not move your old furniture. If you want this done, you will have to negotiate. The reputation of the retailer becomes more important when you deal with the service department. Price is not everything—good service is essential.

Words of Wisdom

Over the years, I have often found it is easier to design a custom piece of furniture for a client. I am fortunate to live in Lancaster County, Pennsylvania, where we are blessed with a wealth of fine craftspeople. Nearly anything I can dream up, they can build, and usually for the same price or very little more than manufactured products. Explore this possibility in your community. You may be surprised. And it is a wonderful feeling to have a one-of-a-kind piece of furniture.

Another place to find interesting one-of-a-kind pieces is a craft show. It's a great place to meet artists from around the country and to explore the "art" of furniture.

BUILT-IN AND ORGANIZED
FURNITURE

As a designer, I adore *built-ins!* I love being able to create something unique that will solve whatever problems the client is facing in terms of storage, space, or design.

Over the years, I have found that most people usually don't even think about built-ins or custom case goods until I suggest it. Even then, they expect that it will be way beyond their budget. In fact, I can usually work within any budget and produce something that will actually better meet their needs than any ready-made piece of furniture.

Built-ins are not a new idea. Actually they are an old idea, brought back to life. The wardrobes and library systems of past eras are now being redesigned and updated for today's living. In the past, they were used primarily in place of closets. But today, they offer flexibility everywhere in the home for a variety of purposes, such as wall systems for televisions and audio and video equipment; storage for books, collections, and clothing; better utilization of closets; a home for computers; and self-contained home offices—the list is endless. The list of styles and finishes for these pieces is just as long.

How do you know when to consider custom-built versus ready-made? If you're even asking the question, then there is a good chance that you should at least pursue the idea. Basically, if you are trying to organize, store, or display a variety of items, then you will probably be happier with something made specifically for your particular use than you would be with something ready-made.

What's next? Find someone you trust! Check the phone book, and then check out the prospective candidates. Go to their shops, talk to previous customers, look at their work. Ask to see drawings and estimates from past jobs. What makes custom built-ins so fun is that virtually anything you can dream of can be produced. Obviously, you need a good cabinetmaker. Over the past several years, I have worked almost exclusively with one firm, Gable Designs—Jeff Gable and his brother Jim. They are terrific and we communicate well. That's so important. Check with interior designers and furniture stores in your area to see if they have ever worked with that particular cabinetmaker. Often, craftspeople specialize in specific styles or categories. So be sure that their area of expertise matches your needs. If someone only does very contemporary work, it will be very difficult for them to do justice to a very traditional style.

One of the first questions asked by a client is, Can I take it with me when I move? The answer is yes. As long as you make this clear up front, before designing or pricing. The basic difference between a system that will be movable and one that is not is that the movable system will be designed more as a modular, with each piece finished on all sides. The system that is built to stay will not be as modular. Instead, it will be in only as many pieces as necessary to get it into the house, without any flexibility, and the backs and unseen sides will not be finished. So there is a difference in price.

 One mistake to avoid—don't think that kitchen cabinet makers are the same as cabinetmakers or furniture builders. Kitchen cabinetry is a different kind of craft than custom-built wall systems or furniture. Some applications are transferrable, but not all. Kitchen people work within certain multiples. Therefore, everything they do must fit a certain basic mold. If you get beyond this, they are then just "making do," rather than "making right!"

Recently, a customer for whom we had built an entire room library system called to say she had decided to build a new, larger home. She wanted to know if we could transfer her library to her new home. Well, we had not planned for this room to be moved. Obviously, it would be a big job and we would have to add to and alter the original piece to fit into a larger room, but it was possible. So we began the process. Then a few weeks later, the client called again to say that the folks who had bought her old home wanted to move in right away! She was thrilled, until we explained that it would be at least two months before we would be able to complete the library for her new home. She wanted to move in two weeks, and she expected that we would be able to meet her deadline! The people I work with are good, but they are *not* magicians. Needless to say, she waited until the library was complete before she moved.

What most people don't realize is that unless you are buying something from a store's stock, you will have to wait six to twelve weeks for any ready-made piece of furniture. So, it only makes sense that you will wait about the same time for custom furniture. Therefore, if you have just missed a cutting and they are sold out, you could wait as long as six months!

Now it's time to begin your basic lesson on construction. Ready?

Basic Construction

MULTIPLES

What are multiples? Well, basically you need to understand that most wood and laminate sheets are made in 4- by 8-foot pieces. Therefore, anything you do is affected by that original 4- by 8-foot size. For example, suppose you wanted a wall system with shelves 16 inches deep. Sixteen inches evenly divides into 48 inches (the 4-foot dimension of the original sheet) three times, so you would need only one sheet for every three shelves. However, if you decided you needed to have the wall system 17 inches deep, you would get only two shelves from each 4- by 8-foot sheet. You would therefore need two sheets for three shelves, so the price will be much higher for 17-inch-deep shelves. This explains why one little inch can make such a big difference. As you can see, there will be a lot of waste with the 17-inch-deep section. So it makes sense to work in multiples of 12, 16, or 24 because they accommodate the most efficient use of the 4- by 8-foot sheets.

What are the standard sizes for basic pieces? Bookshelves on average are 12 inches in depth (front to back). The minimum is 9 inches and the maximum can be 18 to 24 inches deep, but books do get lost and are tough to retrieve when you get this deep. The 18- to 24-inch depth is better for displays or other types of storage.

The widest span (side to side measurement) for a bookshelf is 36 inches or less for wood. If you are using glass shelves, then the span should be determined by the thickness of the glass. For example, use $1/4$ inch thick glass for a 24-inch span, $3/8$ inch thick glass for a 36-inch span, and $1/2$ inch thick glass for larger widths.

Base cabinets vary in depth, the minimum depth being 15 to 18 inches for bookshelves. Audio equipment uses a minimum depth of 20 inches, and for a television you need a minimum of 24 inches.

Heights for base cabinetry usually range between 30 and 36 inches for a standard ceiling of 8 or 9 feet.

PLYWOOD

Don't panic! As with chip core (see Chapter 4), *plywood* is not a dirty word! With today's technology, plywood is actually a superior product than solid wood. It absorbs less moisture and therefore reduces the problem of warping. Because of the nature of plywood, the grain of the wood runs in several directions, which also reduces warping. Wood can only warp in the direction of the grain. So if you layer the grain in different directions, as in plywood, you virtually eliminate the problem of warping. For more information on this, refer back to Chapter 4.

Of course, there are different qualities of plywood. Each has specific characteristics that make it suitable for different kinds of applications.

There are *three basic grades:*

---

1. *Utility*—Used for painted finishes, or unseen inside portions.
2. *Mid grade*—Good quality for inside or outside. This can be painted or stained.
3. *Sequence-matched*—This means that all the 4- by 8-foot sheets came from the same tree, and were cut in sequence. Therefore, the grains will be either identical or continuous in pattern. This is usually stained, and will be uniform in color because the grains match.

The *basic cores* or types of plywood are:

1. *Veneer core*—Basically a "sandwich" of soft wood.
2. *Flake board core*—This is what it sounds like: flakes of wood mashed together. Don't get this wet! It will soak up liquids like a sponge.
3. *MDF* (medium-density fiberboard)—Inexpensive—the most stable plywood and also the heaviest.

Usually a variety of all the above will be used in any given application. So pricing is dependent upon the quality and quantity used.

CABINET CONSTRUCTION

The next item to be determined is whether you want *frame* or *frameless* construction. Frameless is much like what it sounds like: a

CABINET CONSTRUCTION

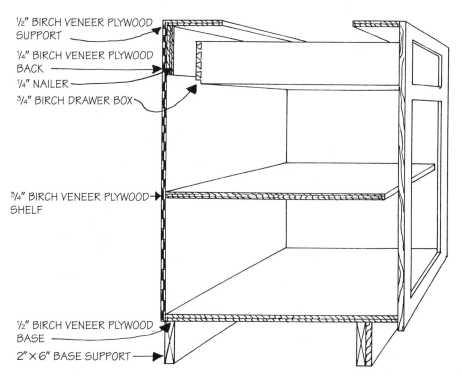

½" BIRCH VENEER PLYWOOD SUPPORT

¼" BIRCH VENEER PLYWOOD BACK

¼" NAILER

¾" BIRCH DRAWER BOX

¾" BIRCH VENEER PLYWOOD SHELF

½" BIRCH VENEER PLYWOOD BASE

2" × 6" BASE SUPPORT

case with doors and no exposed framing around them. This is less expensive than frame construction and is generally more appealing for more contemporary styles.

Frame construction is more expensive and has more structural stability. This type of construction allows for more traditional styling. Each door opening will be individually framed out, with exposed structure between the doors.

You can design a wall system with or without a back. Not having a back will save about $85 to $100 on a 72-inch unit. Having a back will give a more uniform appearance and it is easier than having to clean the marks and scrapes off your wall. Color is also a consideration

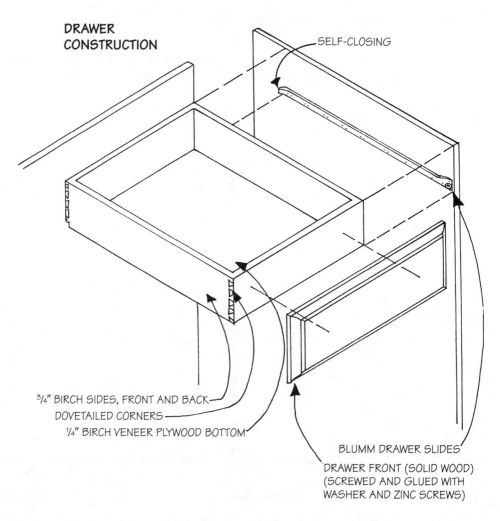

DRAWER
CONSTRUCTION

SELF-CLOSING

3/4" BIRCH SIDES, FRONT AND BACK
DOVETAILED CORNERS
1/4" BIRCH VENEER PLYWOOD BOTTOM

BLUMM DRAWER SLIDES
DRAWER FRONT (SOLID WOOD)
(SCREWED AND GLUED WITH
WASHER AND ZINC SCREWS)

for the back of the unit. If you are planning on a dark color finish for your wall system, you may want to consider a lighter color for the inside back. This will reduce the overall dominating appearance of a large unit.

Doors

Most cabinetmakers prefer to order doors from manufacturers that specialize in doors. Why? Because doors are labor-intensive, unless you can mass-produce them on an assembly line. If your situation or preference is so unique, then a good cabinetmaker can custom-make doors for you. But be aware, this will be a more expensive option.

 It's a good idea to keep the width of each door to 24 inches or less. Once you get much beyond this dimension, you will actually have to back away from the cabinet in order to open the door. So if your dimension requires more than 24 inches, think about going to a pair of doors instead of a single one.

The style of a door will greatly affect the cost. Obviously, the more detailed it is, the more expensive. There are basically two types of doors: *overlay* and *insert*. Overlay doors literally overlay the frame, covering up any inconsistencies. Imagine a flat piece of wood (the door). Now take a picture frame and lay it on top of the original flat door. That's overlay. You can add as many layers as you desire, creating the overall effect of a carved door. Inset doors are individual pieces of wood that fit together more like a jigsaw puzzle. The multifaceted pieces create the illusion of depth, requiring more craftsmanship to execute.

A simpler style of a door is called *lipped*. A lipped door is simply a thick door whose inside face has been channeled or routed out, creating a paneled look. It is effective and reasonable. The thickness of the door is usually 3/4 of an inch—the routing is only 1/4 inch deep.

Pocket doors have become increasingly popular over the past few years. A pocket door will actually slide into the storage area of the cabinet. Once you have opened the door, you can then slide it toward the back of the unit and get it out of the way. The reason for its popularity is the rise in televisions being used in living rooms and great rooms. A door can create a viewing problem for the audience.

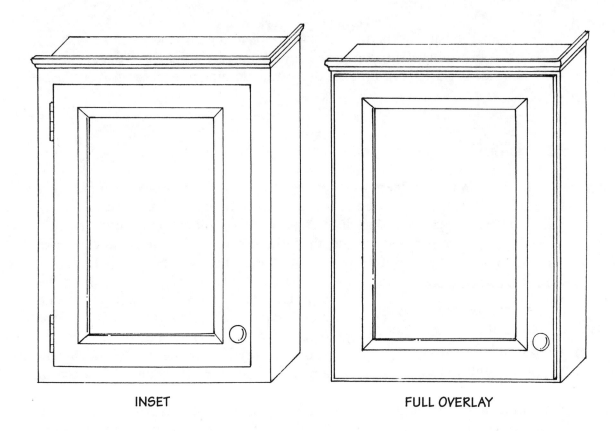

INSET   FULL OVERLAY

Pocket doors work great, but before deciding you can't live without them, be sure you will actually *use* them! I have found that although most people think they are a wonderful invention, they rarely ever close them. Most will just leave them stored in the open position. I guess we all like options! Anyway, here are some constant cost and measurement details of pocket doors.

The hardware required to operate pocket doors costs somewhere between $60 and $80. The doors themselves cost between $100 and $200 per pair for a big screen TV. You will also need to allow about 4 inches more width and depth in your wall unit to fit the doors inside. If you are working with limited space, this can make or break your plans.

While on the subject of televisions, here are some considerations when planning a built-in system for your home theater center.

There are other options for hiding the television such as:

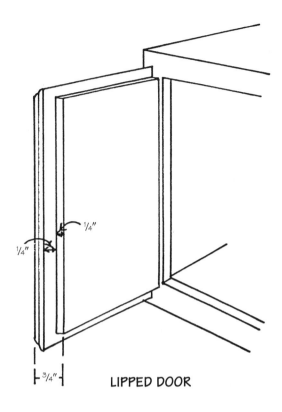

LIPPED DOOR

STANDARD DOORS

It is possible to put your television on a mechanism that swivels and pulls out. This will allow the television to come forward far enough to eliminate the viewing problem of standard doors.

You can choose just a pull-out, which allows you to bring the TV forward, or you can get the combination swivel pull-out. With the swivel, you have the option of turning the TV in the direction you prefer. These units work well, but only for 32-inch or smaller screens.

LAY-BACK DOORS

Lay-back doors open far enough to allow you to lay them flat against the rest of the wall unit. This is great as long as your VCR is not in a section to the side of the television. It is very difficult to use the VCR with a door opened over it.

SLIDING DOORS

Sliding doors are half the dimension of the opening face of the unit that houses the television. So, if you have a big-screen TV, this is not a viable option. However, if you have a smaller TV, then it will be possible. One door slides over the top of the other door, leaving an opening the same size as one of the doors. Complete sliding doors would actually slide out in front of whatever cabinetry is on either side of the television unit. If this is fine with you, these side cabinetry units should be slightly shorter in depth (front to back) in order to accommodate this movement. This type of slider can also be automated. You can get a remote control unit to open and close the sliding door (just what everyone needs—another remote control unit!).

AUTOMATED LIFTS

As if automatic sliding doors aren't enough, imagine having a storage chest at the foot of your bed. You've got your pillows perfectly fluffed, the champagne chilled to perfection, and now it's time for your favorite television show. You certainly wouldn't want to have to move and upset all this luxurious comfort! So don't. Simply push the remote control button on your automated lift and just like magic, the lid of the storage chest opens and the hydraulic lift raises your television from within, to just the proper viewing height! Now this is living.

Considerations for Storing Electronics

Another consideration for any electronic unit, whether it's a television, stereo, VCR, CD player, etc., is ventilation. For televisions, it is not usually a problem, since the doors are open when the unit is on. But for audio equipment, it is an issue. You can create a ventilating hole on the top of your wall unit, or if necessary, you can build a false back and create dead air space behind the unit. Just be aware that you will need to provide breathing room for audio equipment if you plan on operating it behind closed doors. If your wall unit is fitted from floor to ceiling, you may want to have a ventilating grill built in on the front of the unit.

Speakers require some forethought when planning an entertainment unit. Be sure you are allowing for the proper projection of sound. Also, if you are planning on hiding the speakers behind a grill cloth, test the sound before finalizing this decision.

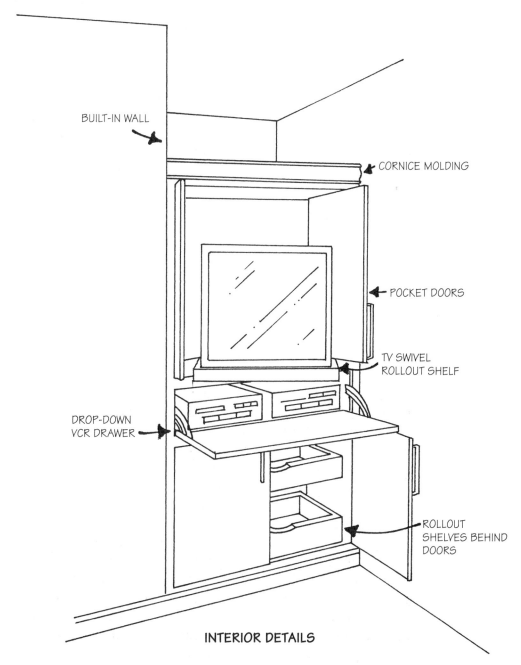

BUILT-IN WALL

CORNICE MOLDING

POCKET DOORS

TV SWIVEL ROLLOUT SHELF

DROP-DOWN VCR DRAWER

ROLLOUT SHELVES BEHIND DOORS

INTERIOR DETAILS

Remote controls are an issue with an entertainment unit. Since most of us use them to operate a variety of equipment, make sure that you have a clear route between you and your equipment. TVs and VCRs are the appliances most operated by remote control. The VCR can be a complex issue unless it is housed in the same space as the TV. For example, if you choose to locate the VCR in a drawer below the TV, consider a hinge on the front of the drawer; this would allow the front of the drawer to drop down so you could reach the electronic eye of the unit with your remote control. You can actually operate an electronic eye through any type of glass, including colored or smoked glass. So this is another option for TVs, VCRs, and audio equipment.

Along with the electronic equipment comes the problem of storing the tapes, CDs, and various knickknacks that go with the equipment. This can be done a couple of different ways. If you prefer to store these items in a door unit, as opposed to a drawer unit, a pull-out storage oranizer can be installed. If you are using a drawer instead, be sure that you have specified a full-extension glide for the drawer, as opposed to the standard three-quarters extension glide. Most kitchen cabinet drawers use the three-quarters glide. With the full-extension glide, you will be able to actually see and use the full depth of the drawer.

Other Interior Accessories

Drawers versus shelves: sometimes you think you need a drawer, but after pricing, realize a door cabinet will be just fine. On average, a 24-inch wood drawer can add $90 to $100 to the cost of the system. It is more functional, but be sure you really need to spend this extra money.

The CD organizer I spoke of earlier costs only about $10 a set. It can be mounted to a sliding shelf and be most efficient. Similar organizers are available for VCR tapes.

If you want a bar unit in your system, you may consider stemware racks or wine racks. For storing liquor, consider a divided drawer.

If you plan on having a refrigerator or ice-maker in your wall system, then purchase this before finalizing the design of the wall system. There are two different types available, under-counter and built-in. Under-counter styles require air space for ventilation.

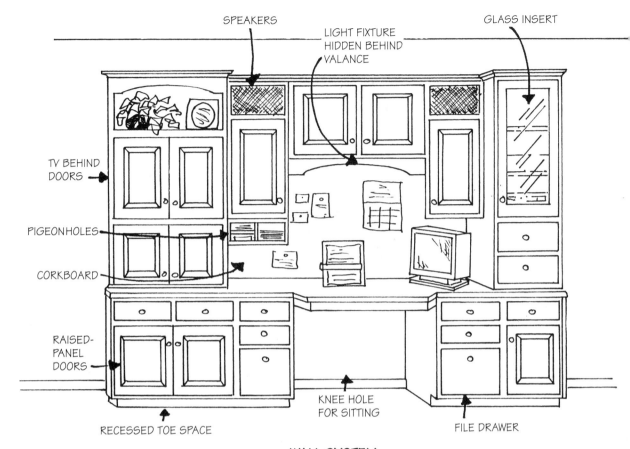

SPEAKERS

LIGHT FIXTURE
HIDDEN BEHIND
VALANCE

GLASS INSERT

TV BEHIND
DOORS

PIGEONHOLES

CORKBOARD

RAISED-
PANEL
DOORS

RECESSED TOE SPACE

KNEE HOLE
FOR SITTING

FILE DRAWER

WALL SYSTEM

Ice-makers come in a variety of sizes and capacities. You may want to purchase a combination refrigerator/ice-maker. A recent client purchased what I think is the world's most expensive ice-maker. It cost $1,175! Good grief, I didn't realize having perfect ice was that important in life!

Lighting

Lighting is another important feature. Almost any unit should have some sort of lighting for practicality. This can be accomplished with a simple incandescent (regular) elongated bulb, discreetly placed inside at the top front of the unit.

If you plan on displaying a collection, then be sure that you use glass shelves, so that the light can filter down through the entire unit.

There are many different types of lighting, and costs vary depending on your choice. Here are the basic types:

1. **Standard incandescent** (usually elongated) bulbs, installed either at the top or back of the unit, behind a small wood valance. This is the least expensive type of lighting.

2. **Canister** or **high hat** lights. This is an incandescent bulb that comes in a variety of wattages and sizes. It is a *flood* style, which means that the upper portion is painted with silver paint on the inside to force the light down, flooding the space below with light. This is the type most used for lighting cabinets. They require about 4 inches of extra height to install, but they do not need any special ventilation for heat.

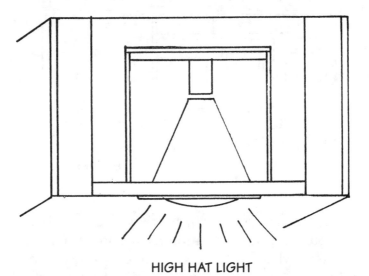

HIGH HAT LIGHT

3. **Halogen bulbs** are relatively new. What makes them unique is that they are tiny, requiring less space. They can be surface mounted in as little as $3/4$ of an inch. However, they get very hot and need about 4 inches of air space for ventilation. They are more expensive than other types of lighting, but the color of light is much whiter than that from standard incandescent bulbs. So if color is a consideration, then this should be your choice.

4. **Fluorescent bulbs** are not used as often as they used to be, but they are still a viable choice. They are practical for display cases because they allow a more even distribution of light. Unlike their incandescent counterparts, which have a beam of light that flares out the farther it gets from the bulb, fluorescent bulbs create more even, focused lighting in a display case. An egg-crate cover is sometimes used as a diffuser to eliminate glare.

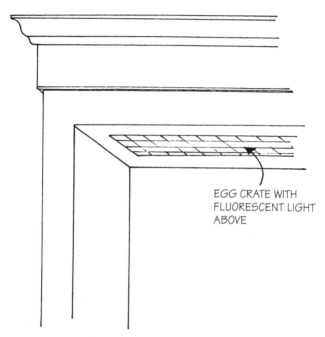

EGG CRATE WITH
FLUORESCENT LIGHT
ABOVE

5. **Strip lights** are tubes with little tiny lights throughout. This creates a very snazzy effect. Again, the distribution of the light is not even, but because it is divided into smaller parts, you can't even tell. Strip lights can be mounted almost anywhere, on the back, top, or even along the sides of a cabinet.

When deciding on lighting, also think about how you will actually turn them on. They can be wired to activate when the door is opened. Of course, that means the light will stay on as long as the door is open. Usually there will be a cord with a switch at the back of the unit. You can also have a surface-mounted switch. This can be a *dimmer* type switch, which allows you to create a dramatic or romantic atmosphere with lighting. If you are using a single elongated bulb, it may have a switch on its housing unit.

Hardware

Hardware refers to the handles or knobs on the drawers and doors and also to the type of hinge used to open and close the doors.

When it comes to door hinges, there are a couple of different types—hidden and not hidden. The not-hidden type can be decorative or functional. Colonial is one style in which hardware such as barrel hinges are not concealed and are decorative by design. Then there is the more functional design called a *knife hinge*, which is recessed into the side of the door. It is discreet because it is small and does not draw attention to itself.

A more expensive type of hinge is called a European or a concealed cup hinge; it is completely hidden because it is installed on the inside of the door. It gives the ability to adjust the angles of the door, and works well with contemporary styles.

Drawer and door pulls are the knobs or handles used to open the doors or drawers. These can range in price from $0.59 to $15. The average price for a good quality brass pull is between $3 and $4. It is well worth purchasing this solid brass hardware because it will last a long time. Brass-plated hardware will begin to tarnish and discolor within a year, especially if it comes in contact with hand lotions or food products. The chemical reactions this causes speed up the process of discoloration.

Of course, you can spend a fortune on more artistic one-of-a-kind pulls. This is becoming increasingly popular. Many craft shows are showing hardware crafted by artisans. It is a way of making your cabinet unique.

Whatever your choice, do take the number and price of pulls required into consideration when designing and pricing a custom-built unit. Most cabinetmakers will assume the $3 to $4 range for hardware, so be sure to discuss all options up front.

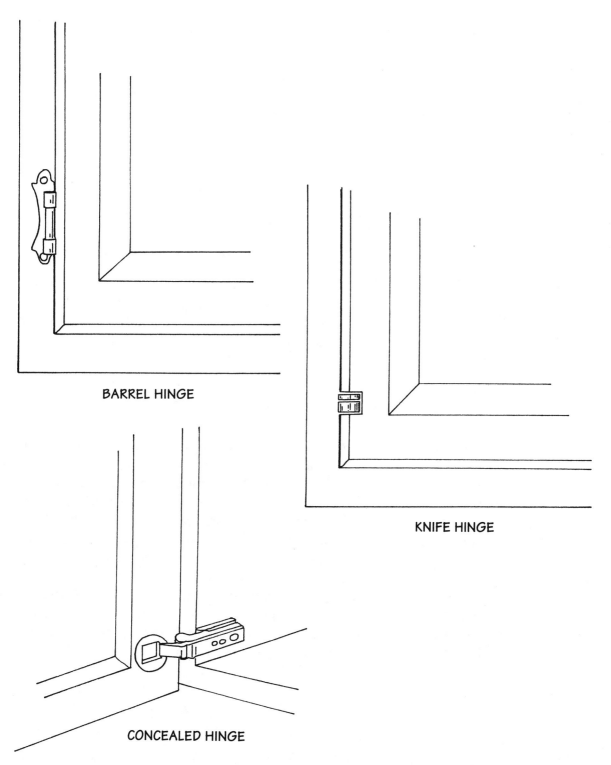

BARREL HINGE

KNIFE HINGE

CONCEALED HINGE

Finishes

Different finishes require different kinds of wood. Obviously, there are also different costs involved. Pine is the least expensive, birch and maple next, oak or white birch follow, and walnut and mahogany are the most expensive. Below are the basic choices for finishes.

PAINT

Do not paint pine or other soft woods. The knots of soft woods will bleed through the finish of the paint. Unless you want to see the knots through the finish, do not use pine. Some country styles do lend themselves to this look, however. If this is your style choice, then it can be effective.

Birch or soft maple are the best choices for painted finishes. They will give a smooth, even finish because their grains are tight. For this same reason, they are not a good choice for staining—the grain is just not very interesting.

STAIN

Pine and the other soft woods will give an informal look when stained. This is suitable for casual style decor choices.

Oak and *white* birch are a wonderful choice for stain. The grain is tighter than pine or soft woods, which allows for more detailed styles. These woods also allow for more flexible stain choices because their own natural color is very light and fairly even. Oak can be bleached to allow for even lighter stains, such as off-white or pastel colors.

Walnut and mahogany are most used for more formal styles. The grain of these two woods is the tightest of all the woods, and because they are darker in color, they stain to a wonderful, rich tone. Mahogany has a natural cherry-wine hue and walnut possesses a rich earthy brown hue. Keep this in mind when deciding which to use.

LAMINATES

These are manufactured plastic materials. Most kitchen counters are made of laminates. Today's technology allows for hundreds of wonderful colors and textures, and laminates are a marvelous choice because of their cleanability and durability. The cost of a laminate finish will depend on the specific laminate used. The basic color laminate will cost about the same as a painted cabinet and increase in price as the detail of the laminate finish increases.

DECORATED AND FAUX FINISHES

Customizing is very popular. You can detail a piece by simply using a combination of colors. Or you can get very fancy with more details such as flowers, or even intricate decorative patterns applied to the finish.

Faux is a French word meaning "false," an imitation. I will discuss faux finishing later in Chapter 6, but the basic idea is to create a finish that imitates something else, usually a texture from nature such as an animal skin, like ostrich or leather. Almost anything you can dream up can be imitated by a good artist in paint. It is great fun to create themes in this way, like in a jungle room. The price will depend on the difficulty of the art.

MOLDINGS AND CARVINGS

Technology has made it possible to get detailed moldings and carvings at reasonable prices. You can purchase moldings and carvings made from foam that can be applied and then finished to match the rest of your unit. Yes, you can also purchase wood carving pieces, but they are more expensive. The only problem with the foam carvings is that they can melt if they get near a flame! Otherwise, it is virtually impossible to see any difference once they are finished.

CUSTOM CARVING/MOLDING DETAILS

THE FINISH PROCESS

Paint

1. Sand and then fill any cracks in the grain to get an even surface.
2. Apply primer—this is sprayed on for the most even coat.
3. Sand again.
4. Apply one to two topcoats of sealer.
5. Finally, after the piece is installed or delivered, do any necessary touch-up.
6. Style to taste. If you have chosen a period or historical style, then you may want to match the brush strokes to an existing surface such as woodwork or trim in your home. If so, then much of this detailing will be finished in your home. If you hire outside help, it will be more expensive, because it is a hand-done technique as opposed to a sprayed finish.

Today's paints provide a much tougher finish than the paints of the past generations. Most paints today are catalyzed lacquer and conversion varnish with pigment added for color. They contain UV blockers to prevent the yellowing of "whites." They will stand up to surface abrasions better, meaning they are more scratch-resistant. And it will usually take several hours before water will damage the finish.

Stain

1. Sand and prep the surface.
2. Apply the stain.
3. Wipe the stain off, to create even absorption.
4. Apply one coat of sealer.
5. Sand again.
6. Apply one to two coats of topcoat.

You can also add detail to your stained finish. One technique is to splatter the stain finish with a darker colored (almost black) stain to

HAND-PAINTED DETAILS

effect an antiqued look. Or you may choose to use two different woods to draw interest not only to their grain contrasts, but also to their color. Different woods take stain differently.

Finding Space

People don't realize just how many unused spaces really exist. When building custom cabinets, there are ways to consider and utilize some of these extra spaces.

Many family rooms back up to the garage. If you choose to build a wall system along this adjoining wall, then you can actually push through the wall if it is not load-bearing. By doing so, the depth of the space the wall system uses in the family room is decreased. This is especially helpful with a large television. Instead of requiring 24 inches or more, it will need only 12 or 15 inches if you can extend it through the wall into the garage.

If you have a Cape Cod home, then use the knee wall to build

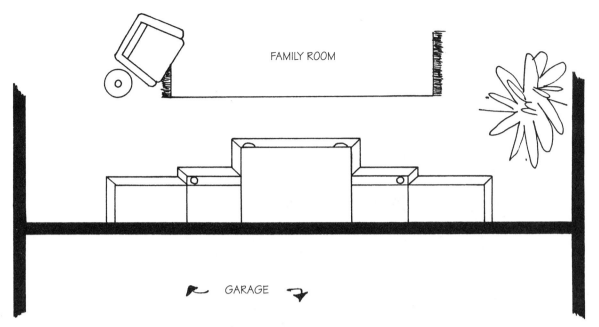

FAMILY ROOM

GARAGE

WALL SYSTEM EXTENDED INTO FAMILY ROOM

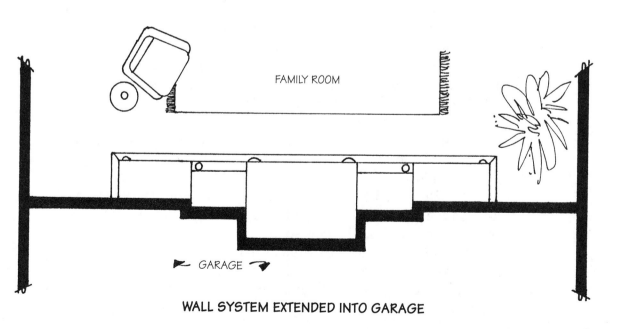

FAMILY ROOM

GARAGE

WALL SYSTEM EXTENDED INTO GARAGE

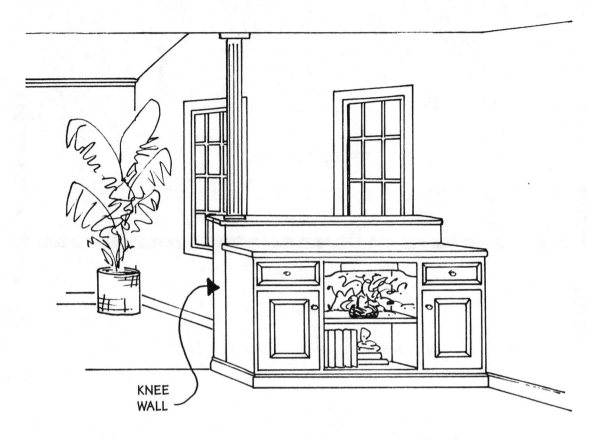

KNEE
WALL

in furniture and cabinetry. This is a great space for clothing storage, bookshelves, a desk, or even a computer space.

Under your staircase is a lot of unused room. This can be a wonderful place to get creative. It's a perfect area for a home entertainment unit, bookshelves, a computer, or displaying a collection.

Take cabinetry up to the ceiling. This is a great place for storage of things used only occasionally.

Check out the dimension behind your bedroom door. If there is a space of 9 inches or more between your door and the adjoining wall, you can build a bookshelf.

One client had an unusually large closet in her family room. We reduced the size of the closet and were able to put a built-in computer desk and bookshelf in the new space.

Add storage for stuffed animals and other toys in a child's room by putting a shelf above the window from wall to wall.

Take a good look around your home, you will be surprised at how much space is just sitting there vacant begging to be designed!

BUILT-IN STORAGE UNDER STAIRS

Words of Wisdom

Plan ahead—it is a lot easier to redraw the plans than to rebuild the cabinet.

When building a large sectional wall system, change the depth of the sections. Put your deepest piece (the dimension from front to back) in the middle and decrease the depth of each adjoining one on either side.

Consider the age of your electronic equipment when planning a wall system. If you suspect you will need to replace something in the near future, go window-shopping now so you know the dimension required for an updated version.

6

WHAT'S ON THE WALLS?

I find it interesting, even amusing, that clients will spend a tremendous amount of time and effort trying to figure out what to do with their walls and then, once the room is finished, never give them another thought.

Actually, this does make sense. Walls are the backdrop for the rest of the room. Thus they should act as a complement to everything else, and not necessarily be the focal point. But that does not diminish their importance. Walls create the overall atmosphere for the artistic display of everything else in the room. Naturally, since the walls compose the majority of the surface area in a room, it is important to get them right.

So, where do you begin? As a designer, I like to put together an overall plan of a space or room, sort of like laying out a road map. That way, I have some idea where I'm going. But unfortunately, reality is far from ideal. And the reality is that I usually have to begin the process somewhere midway through a project. There are many options for your walls, so you must first start by analyzing your needs and your preferences. This is best accomplished with a list of questions.

❀ Do you like wallpaper? Or would you rather have a simpler, plainer backdrop?

❀ Do you like large-scale or small-scale prints? Many people think they like small-scale prints until we get them on the wall. Then they realize they make them dizzy! Be sure to try a large-size sample for several days before purchasing.

* Will you need to wash or scrub the walls often because of little hands?
* Do you have pets with a favorite spot to sleep, leaning up against the wall?
* Are you a fastidious housekeeper? Or do you almost never think about cleaning your walls?
* Think about the traffic areas of your home. Are there areas that will come into contact with moving bodies, hands, and other objects?
* Do you tend to leave the furniture in one place, or do you rearrange it often?
* Are any of your chairs or other movable furniture up close to a wall?
* Do you own a lot of artwork? Do you plan on owning a lot of artwork or other wall displays?
* Do you like open spaces, or comfy, cozy den spaces?
* Do you plan on decorating yourself, or are you going to hire a professional?
* Do you tend to get bored with spaces and like to change them every couple of years?
* What do you own that has to be used in this space?

Obviously, the list could go on forever, so use this just to begin your thought process. After all, once the walls are done, you really do not want to have to move everything out of the room and start all over!

Your basic options are paint, wallpaper, paneling, cork, and tile. But that is just the beginning. It is *what* you do with these elements that makes all the difference.

Paint

I'm not going to get too technical, or attempt to discuss all the chemical properties of paint. But ultimately, it may be necessary for you to spend some time further exploring those areas and specific products, depending on what you are attempting to accomplish with paint. My goal is to make you aware of all the different options you really have when it comes to paint.

THE BASICS

The basic finishes available are flat, satin, gloss, semigloss, and eggshell. Satin is one step up from flat; semigloss is one step down from gloss. And eggshell is a unique soft finish, in between all of them.

This is basically a matter of preference. But I do have one recommendation. If you think you want to use a dark color in a gloss finish, then consider instead using an eggshell finish. The reason is that no wall is perfect, and the gloss finish will magnify every defect on the wall while eggshell will mask them somewhat. If you want to use a flat finish and a dark color, add a little eggshell finish paint to keep it from looking chalky.

OTHER OPTIONS WITH PAINT

At one time, it was just a matter of choosing the color and the finish for a wall. Then things got a little more creative, and trim colors became important. Should you make them darker or lighter than the wall? Hmm!

Today, that is just the beginning. Now you can choose from an entire menu of options such as sponging, striping, bagging, rag rolling, dragging, smooshing, washing, tricolor rolling, texturizing, and shadow painting. Oh, and that's not all . . . you could always have a trompe l'oeil painting, or even stenciling. Maybe a combination of several? Whew . . . I'm tired already!

Most of the above are better known as faux finishing. In some cases, I'm not sure exactly what they are imitating, but none the less, they are interesting. And the majority of these techniques are easy enough for most people to do themselves.

One word of caution—all of these techniques will take patience and time. And they are not the kind of projects you want to tackle if you expect to be interrupted every twenty minutes.

Sponging

Use a sponge with a contrasting color or colors to create a granitelike texture. You can use as many as three colors over a base color without it looking a little busy.

Striping

This can be done by alternating matte and semigloss or eggshell finish paints. You can use the same color paint for a subtle stripe effect or different colors for a more dramatic effect. This technique is especially effective for painting existing paneling (no paint masking necessary to mark the stripes!).

Bagging

Using a plastic bag, you actually remove some of the glaze to create a marbleized effect. Glaze is a combination of paint of your chosen color mixed with a glazing liquid. This produces a transparent paint. I used this technique to refurbish a kitchen in an apartment for a local charity. I painted the old kitchen cabinets a base coat of white. Then I used a soft peach mixed with a glazing liquid and *bagged* just the centers of the doors. It was beautiful and looked expensive but was very cheap to do.

Rag Rolling

This is very similar to sponging except you use rolled rags instead. Make sure you have several on hand.

Dragging

This is similar to bagging, except instead of using a plastic bag, corrugated cardboard is used to literally drag subtle stripes of glaze across the wall. Depending on the direction or directions you drag, the look will change.

Smooshing

Paint a base coat, then use a second color mixed with glazing liquid. While the glaze is still wet, lay a thin piece of plastic against the wet wall. Now, using your hands, smooth it out, wrinkle it, whatever. Then remove the plastic. The overall effect will resemble marble. I prefer to use a darker base and a lighter glaze to accentuate this technique.

Washing

This is the same as smooshing, except instead of using a plastic layer, you use a sponge dipped in glaze and literally wash over the wall. A circular motion works best. This is one of my favorite techniques, especially over a stucco or textured wall. For a true French look, use a stencil pattern to make borders to create the appearance of panels throughout the room.

Tricolor Rolling

This technique uses three different colors of paint on one roller. This is accomplished by using cardboard dividers in your paint tray when you initially pour the paint. Use the roller in an alternating curving motion around the room. When it dries, it looks much like an airbrushed wallpaper.

Note: *For more information on the above techniques,* Minwax *has a video and instruction pamphlet available. Call 1-800-462-0194 for your nearest dealer and further information.*

TRICOLOR
PAINTING

Shadow Painting

Did you ever notice how the sun creates shadows across your walls and ceilings when it comes through the window? Would you like to have that sunny feeling in rooms that don't get the sun? Well, this can be accomplished by using a glaze coat in a shade lighter than the rest of the room. Pencil draw the imaginary shadows that would be created if the sun did shine in your room. Then just paint them with the glaze. It adds warmth and depth with interesting angles. It will definitely pick up your mood!

Trompe L'oeil

This is one of the oldest techniques. It means to "fool the eye." And the greatest examples of this art are in Europe's ancient cities. All the old cathedrals and palaces are filled with trompe l'oeil art. Usually it will be a mural, the size of a wall. It will appear to have columns of marble with wisteria winding around, with a veranda visible opening to a great garden. Let your imagination run wild!

For one of my clients, I actually used a combination of trompe

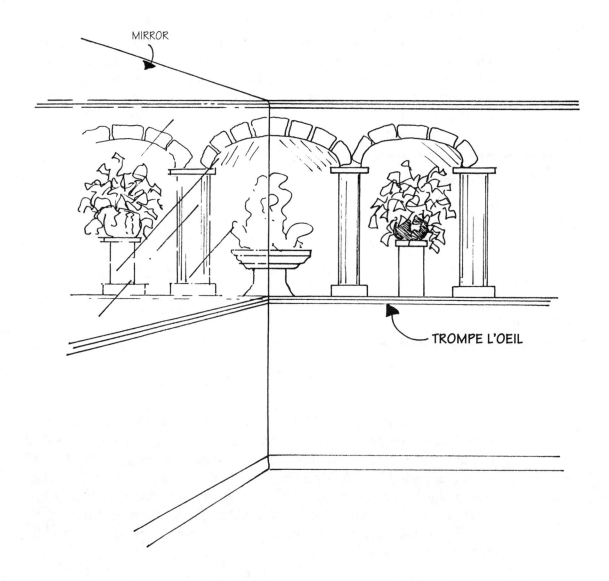

MIRROR

TROMPE L'OEIL

l'oeil and mirrors to create a real illusion. One wall was mirrored completely, from floor to ceiling. Then I had the artist start at the corner adjacent to the mirror. In that corner he began drawing half of a water fountain. Then he added half an arch, and then continued with complete arches and additional details. When the project was complete, the mirror created an optical illusion of a complete water fountain and a complete arch, while also mirroring additional images from within the surrounding spaces. It was spectacular.

Believe it or not, this kind of art is not as expensive as you might think. It has regained popularity over the last ten or fifteen years. As a result, there is a new crop of artists, now accomplished in this technique. I am fortunate to have a wonderful artist to work with—Victor Capecce. He has created open-domed ceilings that expose the sky, birds, and the sun. At night, a galaxy of stars appears in a nursery, or suddenly, a window with a view of the harbor is created where once there was only a wall. Whatever the mind can imagine can be painted, and at a fraction of the cost of the real thing. If you are a do-it-yourselfer, read on. . . .

Stenciling

Most everyone is familiar with stenciling. And depending on your preference, you can add a sophisticated or a country touch with your stencils. But the most interesting new idea with stenciling is to literally stencil a mural (much like trompe l'oeil). This is accomplished with a series of stencils. As many as fifteen or twenty different stencils can be used, depending on the complexity of the mural. A great resource for this kind of product is the Internet. You could try typing in the key word *stencil.*

LITTLE KNOWN PLACES THAT PAINT CAN GO

This chapter is supposed to be about walls. I just thought that while we're on the subject of paint, you would find this interesting.

Did you know that you can paint vinyl flooring, laminate counter tops, and even tile? Well you can! It all comes down to using the right products for the job.

It is possible to make an old neon orange counter top look like granite! Or you can turn that old grungy-looking floor into Mexican tiles! Even plywood can suddenly become marble. If you have the time and the patience, then rid the house of munchkins and go to work! The key is using the right primer so the paint will stick. You may also have to sand the counter top a little first. After painting, use a clear coat sealer for durability. Check with your paint specialist for a list of techniques and products available.

Wallpaper

Choosing wallpaper can be the most overwhelming job in the world. What a helpless feeling, to walk into a store filled with books! Where do you begin?

Well, first of all, don't expect to accomplish this in one day. This is a job that needs time and a systematic approach. The Ink Blot Test in Chapter 1 applies perfectly.

THE INK BLOT TEST

Day One

Scan time. Just like the scan button on your car radio, your job is to take a peek at a lot of different selections from a wide variety of sources. I know it may not look like there is any sense to the way those books are stuffed on those shelves—but there usually is! So do ask for assistance to find your way around.

Day Two

Narrow down your arena. Today you must determine the basic atmosphere of your preferences—contemporary, traditional, colonial, islander, French, Italian, Eastern, or that all-inclusive style—eclectic!

Day Three

By the process of elimination, choose the basic color scheme, pattern, and scale.

Day Four

Now you're getting hot! You can finally begin to choose papers that you would actually consider using. Give yourself a few choices. Then, by process of elimination again, narrow it down to a select few. Now, order a larger sample of each and take them home for a few days. Look at the samples in different light, at different times of the day.

Day Five

Hopefully you are now confident of making the right choice. If not—you will have to start all over again!

RULES ON PATTERNS

Here are some basic rules of the road when it comes to choosing the right pattern for the right space:

❀ If you have a tall narrow room—do not use stripes! They will only make the room taller and narrower. But here is a little technique that will optically bring the ceiling down and allow you to use stripes in a tall narrow space. Place a border on the ceiling, approximately

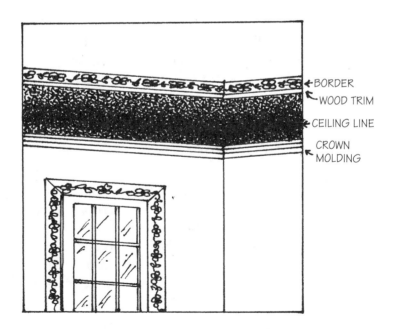

eighteen inches from the wall, then place a second border on the wall, eighteen inches from the ceiling. Now you can either use contrasting wallpaper or paint the space between the border (both wall and ceiling). Then paint the remaining ceiling a second contrast color. The overall effect will be a lower ceiling and a wider space. This will allow the use of a stripe or any other vertical pattern you choose for the walls.

❀ Most people think that they cannot use large-scale patterns in small rooms. However, the opposite is true. A larger pattern can actually create the illusion of more space. Especially if the pattern has an open airy design, such as a large floral bouquet with lots of simple background exposed. And just as the larger scale will enlarge a space, a smaller pattern will shrink a space, particularly if it is a strong colored pattern.

❀ Consider the placement of furniture when choosing a pattern. If in reality very little wall space will actually be exposed, then use a simpler pattern that will basically give warmth and texture. And be careful when using busy tiny patterns. They can actually make some people motion sick! So be very careful. I tend to use those patterns only as fillers below a chair rail or on a ceiling. Anywhere but directly at eye level!

❀ Realize that most of the photographs in the wallpaper books are taken especially to show all the patterns in a collection. This does not mean that most of us could really live with all those patterns together. Be realistic about how much pattern your eyes can really take.

❀ The more patterns, the more chopped up a space becomes. This is great if you have an abundance of space, but awful if you do not. It is also important to consider the number of windows in your room, because they, too, contribute to the cutting up of space.

KINDS OF WALLPAPER

Okay, you now know how to go about choosing the right style of wallpaper. But do you know what kind of wallpaper you want? Have I confused you? Let me explain.

Sometimes wallpaper isn't paper. It can be vinyl, or fabric, or string, or vinyl-coated paper, or woven natural fibers such as rattan or sisal. And choosing the right kind of product is as important as choosing the right style. One more consideration—if you ever plan on removing the wallpaper, make sure it is strippable.

Paper

Most of the more expensive patterns of wallpaper will actually be paper. The reason is that it is the best surface to print on. The cost of a roll of wallpaper will be determined by the extent of detail within a pattern and the number of colors or screens used to produce the pattern. Of course, if you then add the name of a well-known celebrity or designer to the pattern, the price will probably go up even more. Most of these patterns are not "scrubbable," and the more expensive papers will definitely not be prepasted.

Vinyl-Coated Paper

This is basically the same as paper, except that a thin layer of vinyl coating has been added. This paper is called scrubbable, but that doesn't really mean you can scrub it. What it means is that the paper can be gently washed.

Vinyl

Vinyl wallpaper is actually made of vinyl and is paper- or fabric-backed. This is done for two reasons: stability and ease of hanging. The kinds of patterns you will find in vinyl wall coverings are different than paper wall covering patterns. Vinyl does not allow for the same kind of details that paper does. Most vinyls are textured with patterns printed over the texture. They are aesthetic and durable, but they are a different kind of style than paper designs. Vinyl wall covering *is* scrubbable and usually strippable.

Fabric

Fabric wall coverings have a unique richness and warmth. They are usually paper-backed for the same reasons as with vinyl: stability and ease of hanging. With a fabric wall covering you gain durability with detail. However, you will find that most of these fabrics are textured, and the details are as diverse as with regular paper wall coverings. Be sure to check the width of the roll. Fabric wall coverings are often wider—36 inches versus the standard roll size of 27 inches.

String

Actually, this is just what it sounds like. Imagine row upon row of pieces of string glued to a backing. Different thicknesses and colors and backgrounds create interesting textures. Unfortunately, you must accept the fact the edges and cuts will fray and/or peel over time—which can look quite untidy. I do not recommend this with small children or pets!

Naturals

There are hundreds of wonderful natural grasses and reeds that are dyed, woven, and artistically manipulated to create beautiful wall coverings. But like the strings, they can fray and get "picky." So they are not good choices with children and pets. They also tend to get dusty and are difficult to clean.

Commercial

Commercial wall coverings are always vinyl and usually meet flammability and fire codes. They are typically sold in two widths—27 inches and 54 inches. The reason I mention them is they are extremely durable. They are a wonderful choice for areas that will get hard use. Also, the larger width is great for large spaces because it reduces the number of seams. Commercial wall coverings are usually sold by the yard as well as by the bolt.

Wallpaper Borders

Borders are available in all the same varieties as the other wall coverings. With borders, you can create an endless variety of interesting treatments all within your budget. The most commonly used placement of bordering is at the ceiling line or the chair rail line. But there are many more interesting ideas that are simple to do but very effective in adding style to your room.

Try placing a border on the ceiling and an additional border on the wall, leaving a space in between them, like the technique I suggested for tall narrow rooms on page 105. Now you can use either a contrasting color or a wall covering in between. This is especially effective with a high ceiling line or in similar elongated rooms like a bathroom.

Another interesting idea is to dress up a window by placing bordering around it. You can have fun and use two or three borders to create a multidimensional effect. Then by using a simple window treatment, such as a blind or a shade, you can create the illusion of a larger window.

BEFORE YOU ORDER WALLPAPER . . .

Okay, now we have two major areas covered. But you still need some additional information before actually ordering:

❀Most wall covering rolls are 27 inches wide and 4.5 yards long.

❀Most wall coverings are sold only in two-roll minimums. Some companies may allow you to purchase a single roll once you are beyond the first two rolls, but they will charge you a cutting fee. And some wall coverings are sold with three-roll minimums.

The reason for these minimum requirements is that most patterns have a repeat that would make it virtually impossible to get more than one and a half or two cuts out of each roll. As a result, you would have greater waste. With the additional length of a two- or three-roll piece, you have more continuous pattern to work with. And, as a result, less waste.

❀Wallpaper borders are sold either by the yard or by 5-yard bolts. Manufacturers will not cut up a 5-yard bolt. So if you need 7 yards, you will actually need to buy 10 yards.

❀Many of the more expensive papers will need to be trimmed. The salvage edge is left on, and must be hand trimmed. This will make the labor cost more expensive. Be sure when calling for estimates that you find out whether this charge will be applied.

Frequently Encountered Situations

Over the years, there are some situations that reoccur time and again in regard to decorating walls. Here are a few of them.

PANELING

One of the most common questions asked is, What can I do if my walls are paneled? Am I stuck with them? The answer depends on whether or not the wall is finished behind the paneling or just *studded out* (no drywall behind the paneling), and what kind of paneling was originally used—is it real tongue-and-groove planks, or 4- by 8-foot sheets of laminate (pictures of wood)?

If the paneling is 4- by 8-foot sheets and there is not a real wall behind it, you have a few choices.

❀ First, you can take it down and put up drywall. Then you can do anything you'd like.

❀ You can cover it with a nonwoven liner. This amazing product is applied like wallpaper, and it is heavy enough to cover the ridges of most paneling. Then you can go ahead and wallpaper over the liner.

❀ You can use a proper base coat, and then paint over the paneling. You will be amazed at how great a dark ugly wall or even cheap paneling can look with a good paint job. It is particularly handsome in semigloss white. I recommend sanding the paneling and applying a wall-grip primer before painting.

If the paneling is real tongue-and-groove wood planks, such as knotty pine, then you have different options. Usually what most people find objectionable is the wood itself, and not necessarily the texture. So what to do?

❀ A technique I have used often is to literally stain or whitewash the wood with paint. This is done by rubbing the paint into the wood itself. You will need to use a small brush to get inside the open knots. The effect is dazzling. Suddenly, your room will become brighter and cleaner looking. This process can take a while, and you may or may not want to use two coats. I suggest trying a small area, perhaps behind a door first, to learn the technique and be sure you are happy with the results.

❀ There are base coats specifically designed to prevent *bleeding*, but I have not seen this work effectively on knotty pine. The idea is to seal the wood so you can paint over it without the knots or wood stain bleeding through. I would check with a manufacturer's products specialist. Technology is wonderful, and there may be something new and better available soon.

❀ The only other option you have is to either apply drywall over the old paneling, or remove the paneling and start from scratch.

MILDEW

This monster can be a real problem. It can occur not only in warm climates, but anywhere in the world, because these microscopic spores are transported by the wind. And unfortunately, there are no foolproof solutions. However, here is the best I have found:

First of all, do not paint over mildew, as it will come back. Mildew must be removed. To do this, wash the areas involved with a solution of two cups of household bleach per gallon of warm water. It is best to do this a few days before painting. It may be necessary to repeat this process to completely remove the stains.

As soon as the wall is dry, paint it with a good mildew-resistant sealer. Then use at least two coats of a good quality mildew-resistant paint such as Benjamin Moore's K&B. This acrylic, satin-finish paint is very good at resisting mildew even under humid conditions.

WALLPAPER FALLING DOWN

There are a couple of different reasons why wallpaper may refuse to stay on your walls. Either you did not use enough paste or the paste had already dried before you put on the paper. A few other causes might be that you used the wrong kind of paste or sizing (pretreatment product), or your walls were, and continue to be, damp.

Making the Right Choice

Of all the options for your walls, paint is the least expensive and maybe the most flexible. A good paint job should last approximately seven years, and is still the easiest surface to change. A good paint job is one that has good preparation work, with quality brand caulking (to fill in where molding has separated from the wall) and primer, combined with craftsmanship and a good grade of paint. Get recommendations from friends if possible and check out the references of any painter you're considering.

Generally, the more expensive the wall covering, the more expensive the labor to hang it. Why? Because, the costly wall coverings are usually paper and therefore fragile. They also have difficult patterns to match, and therefore require more time to get it right.

Words of Wisdom

There are specific types of paint primer for virtually every type of job. Investigate all your options before beginning to paint. This will make a big difference in the longevity and durability of the job.

Even if the wallpaper you have chosen is prepasted, I recommend using a premixed paste.

Always order at least one extra roll of wallpaper, especially if it is a do-it-yourself job.

Check each roll of wallpaper when you receive it. Look for inconsistencies in the pattern. Check the dye lots to be sure all rolls are from the same lot—do not accept different dye lots, as they will never match. Keep a record of the dye lot and a small sample. If you need to order additional wall covering for any reason, this will make it a lot easier to match.

Most manufacturers will not accept any returns after sixty days. And most will charge a restocking fee, usually 20 percent.

Many wall coverings have matching fabrics. This does not mean that they will match exactly. They are two different materials and they cannot be produced from the same dye lot. So don't expect a perfect match. When in doubt, send for a cutting of the fabric when ordering the paper; that way you can see how they will work together.

When it comes to hanging wall coverings, the biggest mistake made is hanging it upside down! And I have seen many professionals as well as amateurs make this mistake. Always make sure of the direction before sticking it to the wall.

7

WINDOWS, WINDOWS, WINDOWS!

Probably the most difficult design question to answer is, What do I put on my windows? Part of the problem is the reason we have windows in the first place, which is to let light and warmth into the house. So why on earth would we want to cover them up? There are obvious reasons such as privacy, insulation, and, of course, decoration. And if we can figure out the privacy and insulation issues, how can we ever decide what the style or decorative aspect should be?

Because windows are one of the more important design features in a home, when working with a client, I would prefer not to make the choice of window coverings the first item on the agenda. However, because of the privacy issue, it usually is the first item most people want to have decided.

My recommendation is that if you cannot decide on the basic style or character of a room before covering your windows, then choose a temporary or a basic covering to start. There are a couple of different manufactured temporary coverings. They are available in a roll, and are usually made of a nonwoven fiber. You simply pull off the correct size for your window and place it against the glass itself. They are also self-adhesive. A second option for temporary coverings is the old fashioned vinyl roll-up shades. They can be purchased at most discount, do-it-yourself, and department stores. Buy the cheapest available, since this will only be a temporary situation.

Another plan would be to attempt to decide what kind of basic privacy mechanism you would ultimately prefer, such as mini-blinds, shades, or verticals. We will discuss all the different types available later in this chapter.

Before deciding how and how much of a window to cover, let's discuss what a window is supposed to do. The location of a window plays a big part in window covering treatments. For example, a window on the north side of a house in a cold climate should have a window treatment that is designed to insulate and save energy. Windows on the south side should allow as much solar energy as possible to enter the house to make it energy efficient.

Besides letting heat or cold pass through, windows also allow light to enter our homes. And not all windows do this on an equal basis. A double-glazed window (two panes of glass sealed together with an air space between them) allows about 77 percent of visible light in. A window with a high *R-value* or rating will allow about 63 percent of light to pass through. An R-value is a measure of the resistance that an insulating or building material has to heat flow. The higher the number, the greater the resistance. The problem with all this wonderful light is that some of it is ultraviolet radiation. That's the stuff responsible for fading your furniture and carpets and draperies.

To complicate things even further, all of this is relative to the time of year. The sun is higher in the summer and lower in the winter, so the amount of light entering your home will change with the seasons. Oh, and let's not forget skylights! They, too, will affect the ultimate color your home furnishings will become. So you may want to consider window coverings for them too.

So not only do we need to consider the location of the window, but we also have to take a good look at the placement of furniture relative to the windows! No wonder window coverings are such a problem.

And of course, let's say you spent a near fortune on installing that wonderful, huge, two-story window. Why would you ever want to cover it! Unfortunately, most people don't think about window coverings until after they have already installed the windows.

One of my clients built a magnificent home. His intention is that it will pass from generation to generation. So, of course, he put the best of everything into it, including four enormous Palladian (arch-top) windows in the foyer. Unfortunately, any window treatment imaginable for this type of style would be very expensive. Needless to say, it is now four years later and he and his family are still living in a fish bowl.

The world of window treatments is divided into basically two types: *hard* and *soft*. I say *basically,* because sometimes it is difficult to differentiate between the two. I will attempt to make sense out of all this for you. *Hard window treatments* will be covered below; the next chapter will cover *soft window treatments.*

Hard Window Treatments

These include, but are not limited to, horizontal blinds such as mini-blinds and maxi-blinds, vertical blinds, roller shades, woven woods, shutters, pleated shades, twin-cell and triple-cell shades, solar shades . . . and whatever else new technology will create!

Horizontal Blinds

MINI-BLINDS

The world of mini-blinds is very interesting. It is not a surprise to see sale ads offering 50 to 75 percent off. My question is, off of what? Historically, the markup on these products has been astronomical. Because of this, virtually no one has actually been selling at full retail. The fact of the matter is, the industry is trying to straighten this mess out. A new version of consumer-friendly pricing is being developed. My suggestion is to check out all prices carefully.

There are, however, many different qualities of mini-blinds. The least expensive of these are vinyl. The most expensive are aluminum blinds with virtually no visible light gaps.

Mini-blinds have slats that are either $1/2$ inch or 1 inch wide, the most popular of the two being the 1-inch blinds (the $1/2$ inch usually costs more). The slats are threaded together horizontally with strings. Control wands or strings are then used to adjust the angle of the slats to control light. This will allow for complete privacy or an almost unobstructed view of the outside world. You may also pull them up and out of the way. Because they are one of the best ways to control light, they

MINI-BLIND

are very popular. They can be used alone or with a decorative window treatment.

Vinyl Mini-blinds

These inexpensive blinds are rarely available in custom sizes, which is fine if your window is a standard size. One of the biggest problems with viny mini-blinds is that they react to temperature changes. In other words, if they are on a south-facing window and receive a lot of sun, they will warp. And once they warp, there is nothing you can do about it. Another problem is that they will not hold up to the torment of a child, cat, or dog trying to see the outdoors by bending the slats and sticking a head through them. They will ultimately maintain the bend. Color will also change over time with a vinyl mini-blind.

PVC Mini-blinds

Blinds made of PVC are stronger and of better quality than their vinyl counterparts. Some manufacturers guarantee that PVC blinds are completely warp- sag-, scratch-, and bend-resistant. They also claim these blinds will remain consistent in color even after years of exposure to harsh sunlight. If you can find these wonder-blinds they may be the perfect option for those spaces with small children and pets. Unfortunately, not many retailers carry them.

Aluminum Mini-blinds

These come in a variety of prices. The least expensive aluminum models are thinner and usually have limited color choices. Almost all aluminum minis can be custom sized. The price of the aluminum mini goes up as quality and features increase. Some of the features and options are better mechanisms, more color choices, thicker aluminum slats, multicolor options, size of the holes in the slats (where the string threads through), and the type of *valance* (or head railing) used. You will also be able to choose strings versus wands for controlling the up, down, and tilting movement of the mini-blind. Some are available with "perforated" slats. This creates a wonderful shielding effect while still allowing you to see out. The more expensive mini will also allow you to choose a neutral color for one side of the slat and a true color for the other side. This makes it possible to use bright, wonderful colors inside and maintain a neutral exposure for the exterior of your home.

Wood Mini-blinds

These blinds are more expensive than aluminum. And again, there are a variety of prices available. The basic differences are the same as with the aluminum blinds. The thinner the wood slat and the fewer the stain or color choices, the less expensive the blind. The problem with wood blinds is that because they are a natural material, they react to humidity and temperature. It is common for wood blind slats to warp. However, most manufacturers will replace the warped slat at least once. I suggest you order extra slats if you are placing wood blinds in a very sunny window. That way, with some direction, you can replace the slats yourself when necessary. Wood blinds are available in painted, stained, and sandblasted (paint) finishes. You may also have a choice of slat styles such as square or rounded corners.

Fabric Mini-blinds

Fabric mini-blinds are not as popular as the other varieties we have discussed. I know of only one manufacturer that is producing a regular line of fabric minis. They are made of a wonderful textured fabric and a stiffener is applied to create the slats. They have a casual, cozy feel to them.

Custom Fabric Mini-blinds

This is a wonderful option. With these blinds you choose a fabric and then have it laminated to an aluminum mini-blind. It can be very effective. However, I warn you that it also can have its problems. After time, you may notice fraying on the edges, indicating delaminating or lifting of the fabric.

Sunglass Mini-blinds

The brand name of this product is Optix. These blinds are plastic slatted shades that act much like a pair of sunglasses. Optix transparent blinds eliminate nearly 100 percent of the sun's ultraviolet rays. They come in a variety of shades, such as gray, bronze, black, gold, and hazel. They allow you to see outdoors while shading the glare of the sun but they will not give you complete privacy. They are fairly expensive, but well worth it if you have a major sun problem and would still like the view.

MAXI-BLINDS

Maxi-blinds are mini-blinds with bigger slats. Slats for maxis are available in 2-inch and 3-inch sizes. The 3-inch size is usually reserved for wood blinds. With maxi-blinds, you have one more option than with minis. The string that threads through the slats of a blind is called a *ladder*. On a larger slatted blind, it is possible to use a larger ladder, such as a ³/₄-inch solid cloth tape, or a 1¹/₂-inch solid cloth or decorative tape. You can choose this ladder to match or contrast the color of your blind.

Rigid Polymer Maxi-blinds

These blinds are a recent development. They look much like wood, with a grained texture, but are perfect for use in places where wood would never dare to go—the bath or shower! They are moisture resistant and virtually indestructible. They are also available with a cloth tape ladder.

OPTIONS

Many of the above blinds are available with two blinds under one valance (headrail). This is perfect when you have two windows framed together. You will not get as much of a gap between the blinds as you would with two separate headrails, and it is a much more attractive installation.

Extension brackets allow you to install blinds on the wall above a window's frame and still clear it. That way you won't have it rubbing against your window frame.

Dust-resistant finishes are becoming more readily available. Dust has been the biggest drawback of metal blinds. But remember, those blinds aren't dust-free, just dust-resistant.

Control or wand positions allow you to select right- or left-handed operation of the blind. I usually choose the side that will allow me to hide the controls under a drapery treatment if one is being used along with the blind.

Hold-down brackets will keep the blind in place on a door. There is nothing more annoying than the continuous rattle of a blind banging against a door.

Cutouts are needed if you have an obstacle that blocks part of a window. You will need to make a diagram or template for this in order to get a close fit.

Vertical Blinds

Vertical blinds are vertical slats, either 2 or 3½ inches wide, the most popular size being 2 inches. They are attached to a headrail or valance, and for certain applications they can also have a channel or rail at the bottom. Sometimes they are attached to each other at the bottom by a chain. The angle of the vertical slat can be adjusted to control light. And much like horizontal blinds, you can adjust them from a completely closed to an open position.

Vertical blinds are most often used for sliding doors because they have the ability to *traverse*. Traverse means to travel, or move. In the case of verticals, they can move to the side like a pair of draperies. You can either move the entire width of slats to one side or split them in the middle, so that half moves to the right and the other half moves to the left side of the door or window.

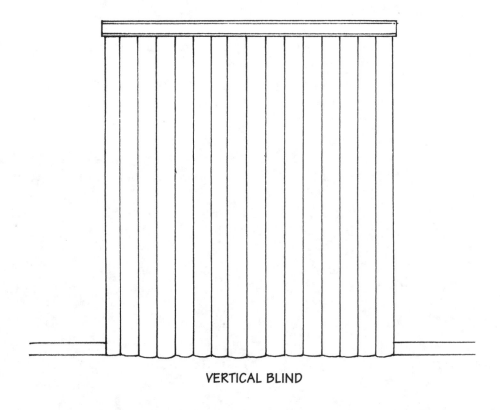

VERTICAL BLIND

If you want to use vertical blinds to cover large areas, I suggest having them motorized. Motorized verticals are controlled by a remote control unit. If you live in a tropical location, you may want to consider a photosensitive eye/motorized mechanism. This controls the blinds as the sun changes position during the day, without you having to move a muscle.

Another common application for verticals is for wide expanses of glass windows or glass walls. Like mini-blinds, verticals can be used alone or in conjunction with other decorative window coverings.

The basic factors affecting the price of vertical blinds are the quality of the operating mechanism, the kind of fabric or material used for the slats, the size of the window, and the number of options and/or colors available.

MECHANISM

The best-quality mechanism uses a *wheeled* system. This allows for smooth traversing, 360-degree rotation of the individual slats, auto-rotation, and reduction in stacking space. Smooth traversing means the slats won't get jammed up or require a weight lifter to operate them. With 360-degree rotation you have more control of the light entering the room.

Before you can traverse vertical blinds, you must make sure they are in the "open" slat position. This means you can see out through them. If they are in the "closed" position, they will jam and not operate. Auto-rotation means that they will automatically rotate themselves to this position each time you attempt to traverse them.

Stacking space is the amount of space needed when the verticals are traversed open. For example, if you chose to have your verticals traverse to one side, then all the slats would move to the side of the door. The amount of room they now occupy is called stacking space. With a more expensive mechanism, they can move closer together, thus using less stacking space. This is important when you are trying to allow for maximum window exposure when the blinds are traversed.

Another upgrade option is the kind of control wand or chain used. The standard method is a chain control. There are two chains, one for rotating the slats and the other for traversing the slats. There are two problems with this: you never know which one is which, and because the chains are actually one continuous piece, a noose is formed, which is dangerous for children and pets. For these reasons, I prefer the wand control. With this type, you twist the wand to rotate the slats and pull it to traverse the slats.

FINISHES

Solid Vinyl

Vinyl verticals are the least expensive. They are also durable and easy to clean.

Flat/Curved. The basic vinyl vertical is available in a flat-slat version and a curved-slat version. The curved slat gives a softer look. I also think it holds its shape better. Flat slats usually end up twisted after time.

Sculpted. The slats of sculpted verticals are available in several different shapes. These shapes can create the effect of undulating waves or an optical illusion of layering. This style is appropriate for more contemporary spaces.

Textured. Textured vinyl slats are available in a variety of styles. They may be ribbed or have mini-perforations throughout. Basket weave is another popular texture.

Pearlized. Pearlized slats have a soft iridescent finish.

Fabric

Polyester. There are hundreds of different fabrics available for verticals. The majority are made of a polyester fabric. It is durable and fade-resistant, which makes it very practical for this kind of an application. It feels and looks more like woven plastic than actual fabric.

Because of its stability and stiffness, polyester can be used for "free-hanging" slats. With other fabrics, such as cotton, a plastic sleeve or *groover* (see Other Fabrics) must be used in vertical slats.

There are many different colors and weave patterns availabe in polyester. Prices vary with selection.

Other Fabrics. Almost any fabric or wallpaper can be made into verticals. This is done with the use of a groover.

A groover is a plastic slat with channels on one side. Your fabric or wallpaper choice can be inserted into this channel. One side of the slat will then be plastic and the other will be your custom fabric.

Metal

Aluminum is the metal of choice—it's not a heavy metal! There are hundreds of colors to choose from. At one time, metal was the only choice for verticals.

Macramé

Macramé looks exactly as it sounds—like macramé. It's a kind of crocheted look. One of the problems with this style is its stability. The slats have a tendency to "grow" or get longer as time goes by.

OPTIONS

Valances

There are many different valance styles available for verticals. Depending on the brand you choose, you may or may not have to pay for a valance.

If a valance is not included in the pricing, then you should ask if a *channel cover* is included. The channel is the aluminum rail of the mechanism. A channel cover is simply a piece of the slat fabric cut to fit as a cover for the channel.

Some valances have a *dustcover* option. A dustcover is basically a top for the valance, to keep light and dust out.

The latest style in vertical hardware is a decorator rod. Similar to those used for draperies, it is available in wood and brass finishes.

Roller Shades (Not to Be Confused with Roller Blades!)

You probably already know what these are. They are typically white vinyl shades that can be purchased in any discount or hardware store. But that is just the beginning of the story.

Roller shades have recently become popular again. And as a result, the choices and styles they are available in have been greatly expanded.

The basic shade now comes in a choice of colors (mostly pastels), a choice of textures and finishes, and a choice of privacy levels, such as opaque or complete blackout (for those people who must have complete darkness for sleeping).

And you will find varying prices, based on the quality of the operating mechanism.

OPTIONS

❀ Regular or reverse roll. In other words, do you want the shade to roll off the front or back of the roller?

❀ Bottom-up operation—in other words, mounting the shade on the window sill so it can be pulled up toward the top of the window. Because of its uniqueness, I use this type of installation often, and it is also available on other types of shades that we will discuss later.

❀ Bead chain operation. A chain is added for pulling the shade (rather than pulling with your hand on the bottom of the shade to operate it).

❀ Decorative pulls. A little handle can be added to the bottom of the shade so you don't have to pull the shade itself to operate it.

❀ Scalloped bottom. You can choose a decorative hem rather than a simple straight bottom.

❀ Custom laminated shades. You can choose your own fabric and have it laminated (glued) to a roller shade. This can also be done with wallpaper, although in my experience, the wallpaper eventually unglues!

MOUNTING

When measuring for roller shades, you must decide exactly where you are going to mount them—inside or outside the window.

Inside Mounting

The width of the shade is measured tip-to-tip (the tip being the end of the metal node that inserts into the mounting hardware). Measure the width of your window at the top, and do not make any deductions. Shades will automatically be made $1/8$ inch narrower. The actual shade or cloth will be $5/8$ inch narrower than the tips of the shade.

Height is measured from the top of the opening (inside frame) to the window sill. The factory will add extra fabric to permit shades to be fully closed.

Outside Mounting

The width will be determined by where you decide to mount the shade.

If the shade is to be mounted outside the window trim, measure to your desired coverage and add $1 1/4$ inches to the width (for shade tips).

For height, measure to the sill. If you are mounting the shade above the window frame, add 3 inches.

WOVEN WOODS

Woven woods are roll-up shades made of natural fibers, usually basswood. They are woven into either Contemporary- or Early American–style patterns, using extra-heavy seine twine. They operate on a pulley system for rolling the shade up, and are mounted with screw and eye hangers.

They are available in a variety of finishes such as natural or unfinished, stained, custom colored, lacquered, and privatized (which means they have a backing).

The thickness of the wood used will determine the overall pattern. My favorite is a simple matchstick pattern (very thin strips woven together with a cotton thread) in a natural color. This will work with most decorating styles.

Woven woods are relatively inexpensive—for example, a shade 36 inches wide and 60 inches long retails for about $160.

Shutters

Shutters are one of my favorite window coverings. I especially like the large-louvered Plantation-style shutters. Which only makes sense, since I would prefer to be living in the Caribbean Islands, and this is the most popular window covering there. Unfortunately, shutters are one of the more expensive options available.

Of course, you can find rather inexpensive, durable, assembly-required brands in the DIY stores. *DIY* is an industry abbreviation for "do-it-yourself." But to get the best quality shutters in custom shapes and sizes with any kind of finish you can imagine, you must go the special-order route. And if you decide to spend the money for good shutters, then spend the extra dough needed to have them properly installed. Installation makes a world of difference with shutters.

Shutters are basically available in two types of materials; wood and vinyl polymer. The vinyl polymer shutters are a recent development. They are wonderful for those places where wood would not stand a chance, such as the bathroom.

They can be adapted to fit a wide variety of challenging window situations, such as French doors, sliding doors, arch-top windows, casement windows, and most standard windows, of course. They can be double-hung, bayed or bowed, bifolded on a track, bypassing on a track, or fixed. They can be used as swinging cafe doors or hung in a skylight.

CONSTRUCTION

The options and style choices for shutters vary from manufacturer to manufacturer. I will attempt to cover the basics of shutter construction.

Louvers

These are the slats on the shutter. They can be vertical or horizontal in style. The slats are usually made in five sizes: $1\frac{1}{4}$ inches, $1\frac{3}{4}$ inches (flat), $2\frac{1}{2}$ inches, $3\frac{1}{2}$ inches, and $4\frac{1}{2}$ inches (tapered).

Panels or Frame

All four corners of a well-made shutter will be doweled and glued. (A *dowel* is a round pin that fits into holes in adjacent pieces.) Adjoining panels should be *rabbeted* to prevent light gaps. (A rabbeted joint

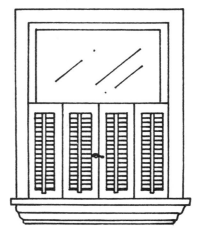

HORIZONTAL LOUVERED SHUTTERS

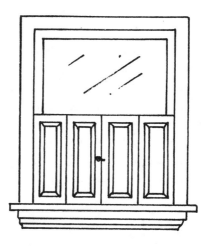

RAISED-PANEL SHUTTERS

has a deep notch near one edge of a board so that another board can be fitted into it.) Outer hinges should be *mortised* (a slot is made in a piece of wood joining it to another) into the *stile* (or edge).

If louvers are not your style, shutters are available with fabric panels or decorative wood-raised panels.

FINISHES

Most quality manufacturers will have a large selection of colors available at a standard price. They will also offer custom color choices.

BASIC RULES FOR SHUTTERS

❀ Use as few panels as possible to cover your window. This will allow for maximum visibility and light control.

❀ Do not use panels larger than 48 inches—they get to be too cumbersome to handle. Try not to hinge together more than three panels; if you do, it will be difficult to keep them from sagging at their points of connection.

❀ If your space is larger than 96 inches, you will need to add additional framing for support. Use a post attached as a permanent fixture.

❀ If your windows are almost the same size in one room, then attempt to use the same size shutters for all windows. This will allow for the same number of louvers, etc.

❀ Unless you are a skilled cabinetmaker, I do not recommend measuring or installing shutters by yourself. Let the retailer you are ordering from do all the measuring. Be sure they have ordered all the necessary equipment for installation.

Pleated Shades

Pleated shades were revolutionary when they were first introduced in the 1980s. Originally only available in a polyester fabric and in limited color choices, they are now made in hundreds of different varieties.

Pleated shades are made of relatively thin fabric that is fanfolded. This allows the shades to be very compact when in the "open" position. For this reason, they are very popular. They also work well with or without other window coverings. I particularly like to use them instead of a sheer drapery under decorative treatments. A lace fabric pleated shade works well with traditional styles.

Originally designed specifically to control the heat transference of the sun, they were and still are available with a metallic silver backing. This backing reflects the sun so that it does not filter through to your home. Because the silver backing changes the colors of the shades themselves, making them appear grayer in tone, it is not recommended for light colors.

BASIC CONSTRUCTION

The headrail (what the shade is attached to) is $1^1/_4$ inches deep and $^5/_8$ inch high. The bottomrail (what gives the shade weight to keep it in place) is $1^3/_{16}$ inches deep and $^1/_2$ inch high. They are made of roll-formed steel and usually have a baked enamel finish.

Pull cords are made of shrink-resistant polyester. You can choose whether you prefer right- or left-handed operation.

The usual minimum width available is 6 inches and the maximum is 144 inches. Maximum height is 96 inches. Some fabrics may have further restrictions on size, so before getting your heart set on a specific fabric, find out if it is available in the size you need. A word of caution for large shades: they tend to sag in the center. Also, with larger installations, the fabric will have to be seamed. If you need to use a shade with seaming, ask for a layout of where the seams will be. You do not want to be surprised.

OPTIONS

❀ Basic fabric choices are sheer, semisheer, privacy, blackout, opaque, and metallic. Pleated shades are antistatic and repel dust. To clean, use a vacuum brush. They can also be sponged with tepid water and mild suds if necessary. Do not use cleaning products on these fabrics.

❀ Pleated shades can be made as *bottom-up* shades, which means you can mount them on the window sill and pull them up toward the top of the window. The advantage to this type of installation is that you can accomplish privacy by covering the lower half or three quarters of the window. And you can leave the upper portion of the window "open" to let the light in.

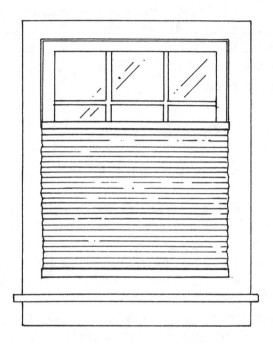

BOTTOM-UP SHADE

❀ Arch-top and half-arch styles are available and are often operable (which means you can actually open and close them) as opposed to stationary. If operable, they will be mounted on the bottom sill and pull up toward the top.

❀ Crank-style skylight pleated shades mounted with tension strings are another option. The shade is pulled along the tension strings with a crank pole.

❀ Liners are also available. This is very effective if you are using a lace pleated shade and want to add privacy or color with a lining installed behind the shade.

❀ Borderline trims are a great way to customize your shade.

❀ A two-on-one headrail is great when you have two windows framed together.

❀ Slant-top shades work in triangular windows.

❀ Hold-down brackets should be used if you are installing a shade on a door. They will keep the shade from banging every time someone uses the door.

Twin-Cell (Honeycomb) Shades

I love *twin-cell* shades. They are very similar to pleated shades, except that two layers of fabric are joined at the top and bottom of each pleat. A side view looks much like a honeycomb. These shades are great insulators and create a beautiful decorative look. The overall effect is soft and almost cloudlike in appearance. They are perfect in almost any style room. And like the other hard window treatments, they work well alone or with other decorative window coverings.

The only disadvantage is that they either are *open* or *closed*. Yes, you can open them partially, but you cannot tilt the pleats to control light.

They are made of a nonwoven polyester fabric that is permanently pleated. Regardless of the color you choose, the street side (the part exposed to the exterior) will be white. The color will appear more intense if a shade is partially open.

Honeycomb shades are available with two different-size pleats, $3/8$ inch and $3/4$ inch. The size you choose should be appropriate for the scale of your window.

Like the pleated shade, they are antistatic and repel dust. You should vacuum them with a brush on occasion. And when needed, you can sponge them with tepid water and mild suds (use the sudsy part, not the water part! You do not want to saturate these shades with water because you can permanently remove the pleats).

Honeycomb shades cost more than single-fabric pleated shades, but I think they are worth it. They provide better insulation and more privacy, and hold pleating better. Besides, I just find them more attractive.

CONSTRUCTION

The color of the headrail and bottomrail coordinates with that of the shade. The rails usually consist of an enamel finish on aluminum. Pull cords are shrink-resistant polyester. You may choose right or left cord installation.

The minimum width is 6 inches and the maximum width is 144 inches. The maximum height is 144 inches. Again, like the pleated shades, "settling" or "sagging" is natural. If you continuously leave the shades extended, you can expect some settling—which means the pleats will be slightly fuller at the bottom than at the top. This is not a defect and, in fact, can look very elegant.

The stacking dimension will vary from fabric to fabric but is usually about 2½ inches for a shade with a length of 72 inches.

FABRICS

Honeycomb shades are available in many solid colors and patterns. You can choose from a few different privacy levels such as sheer, privacy, and blackout. The blackout shade will make the room dark! So if you are planning on using the shade for privacy, be sure you don't unintentionally eliminate all light. You will know if it is day or night with the standard fabric, as it will filter light through it.

MEASURING AND INSTALLATION

Window Shades

You can install honeycomb shades inside the frame of the window or outside or at the ceiling.

Inside Mounting. This requires a minimum recess of 1⅝ inches for the ⅜-inch pleat, and 2¼ inches for the ¾-inch pleat.

The width should be measured in three places on your window—top, middle, and bottom. Use the narrowest dimension. The shade will be ⅜ inch narrower than this dimension, so it will not rub against the window casing or get stuck on it.

The height is not as critical for accuracy. In most cases, the shade will rest on the window sill. If this is your desire, then add ¼ inch to the height measurement.

Ceiling Mounting. The width should be the exact measurement you wish to cover. It is recommended that the shade overlap the opening of the frame by 1½ inches on each side or extend ¼ inch beyond the side trim or casing.

The height should be measured from the ceiling to the sill, apron, or floor. If the window has no trim, measure to a point approximately 1½ inches below the opening.

Mount the shade directly into the ceiling, but be sure you anchor it well. If you are not fortunate enough to have hit a stud or another cross member in the ceiling, then be sure to use anchors. I prefer the heavy-gauge plastic or metal screw-type anchors. They look enormous, but they work very well.

Outside Mounting. On ⅜-inch pleats, the headrail will project 1⅝ inches. On ¾-inch pleats, it will project 2¼ inches.

The width should be the exact measurement you want covered. It is recommended that the shade overlap the opening by 1½ inches on each side or extend ¼ inch beyond the window trim or casing.

The height should be measured from the top of the trim to the sill, apron, or floor, depending on your preference. If you intend to mount your brackets above the window trim, then you will need to add 1½ inches to this measurement. If your window has no trim or casing, add 3 inches for overlapping the top and bottom.

If you want the shades to open enough to clear the glass completely, then add the stacking dimension to your overall height.

Skylight Shades

Measuring and mounting skylight shades is a bit more difficult. It is preferable to have a professional handle this, but if you insist, here are the basics.

First a word of caution: skylight shades need 4 inches of clearance between the glass and the shade to prevent excessive heat buildup. If there is not enough space, an air-pocket barrier will be created and the heat of the sun will become trapped. This can cause the shade to actually singe or burn.

Also, if the mounting surface is not at a 90-degree angle to plane, you will need to use shims to mount the brackets.

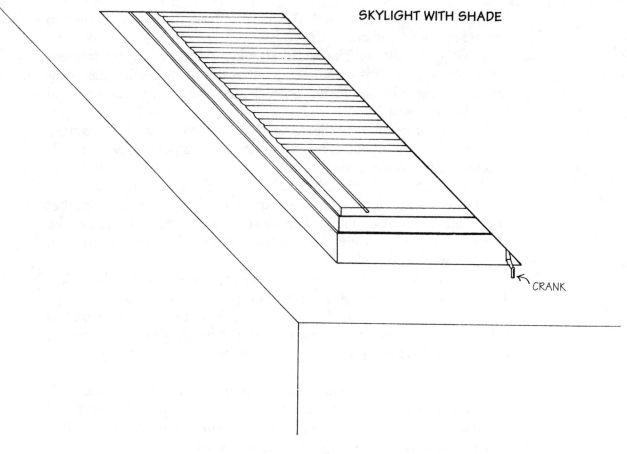

CRANK

Inside Mounting. The width of the opening should be measured in three places: at the top, middle, and bottom. Use the narrowest dimension. Unless you specify otherwise, the manufacturer will make a reduction allowance of $1/4$ inch to prevent the shade from rubbing against the frame. The height is the simple measurement of the opening.

Outside Mounting. The width for outside mounting is the measurement of the opening. If the window has no trim, add $1^5/8$ inches to each side for overlapping of the opening. If the window has trim, add $1/2$ inch on each side.

The height measurement is determined by adding the height of the opening plus $1^5/8$ inches for each side for the stationary rails. If you want to open the shade enough to clear the glass, add the stacking dimension to the previous total.

The most important part of installing skylight shades is making sure you have a ladder that will actually reach to the ceiling!

OPTIONS

A unique option for honeycomb or twin-cell shades is called a *doublefold*. This means the shade is divided horizontally, and has the option of opening from the top down or the bottom up.

A second unique option is called Daylight Doublefold. It's really two shades in one—a sheer material and a privacy fabric sewn together at the bottom. You have the ability to operate the shade from the bottom up or the top down. The direction you choose to open the shade will determine which fabric will show, so you can choose the sheer fabric for daytime and the privacy fabric for night.

Other options includes:

❀ Slant tops
❀ Two-on-one headrail
❀ Hold-down brackets and extension brackets
❀ Skylight crank-style shades.
❀ Upgrade hardware mechanisms. Most manufacturers offer them, which is important if you are using a heavy, large shade.
❀ *Duette Vertiglide*. This is essentially a shade turned on its side, so it can open from side to side. This is appropriate for sliding doors, and you may choose to open the Duette Vertiglide to one side or have it split in the middle.

TRIPLE-CELL SHADES

Triple-cell shades are exactly the same as twin-cell, except they consist of three layers of fabric. The advantage is that they provide more insulation.

The disadvantage is that they require more room to install, so they are difficult to mount on the inside of a window. And of course, they are more expensive than twin-cell shades.

Triple-cell shades are not as popular as other varieties. Because of this, the fabric selections are not as varied. The installation requirements and measurements depend on the specific fabric you choose.

Silhouette Shades

Silhouette shades are one of the most exciting products to hit the market in many years. They consist of soft fabric vanes (or slats) floating between two separate pieces of sheer fabric. This unique construction allows you to control light as with a blind, by rotating the angle of the vanes. At the same time, it has a refined, elegant look like sheer draperies. In the "closed" position, Silhouettes can be rolled up like other shades. They have a self-contained valance that the shade rolls up into. The sheer facings provide a soft filtered effect when the vanes are in the "open" position.

COLORS

The vanes are available in a palette of designer colors, from rich jewel tones and earthy midtones to soft, subdued, misting colors. The exterior sheer is a soft white that will take on whatever color you choose for the vanes.

CONSTRUCTION

The Silhouette operating system has a single continuous cord that raises and lowers the shade. This cord also operates the tilting of the vanes. The bearings are self-lubricating and easy to operate. The clutch mechanism, which holds the shade in the position you desire, is spring-loaded. The headrail is made of a color-matched aluminum.

Silhouette shades can be made in widths from 12 to 96 inches and heights up to 96 inches. They can be mounted either inside or outside the window frame. They are deeper than ordinary blinds, so the headrail will protrude further. But because of the headrail's sleek design, this is usually not an objection.

Despite the soft, gentle appearance of these shades, they are quite durable. And they are one of the few products with a five-year limited warranty.

Although this is one of the nicer shade looks, it is more expensive than most of the other options we have discussed. But it is unique in style and operation. A few words of caution though—if you own cats that are not declawed, do not use this product anywhere that they can reach! They will find the sheer fabric irresistible. When they glide their little nails across this fabric (or any other sheer fabric), it makes a wonderfully annoying sound that cats cannot seem to resist. And I guarantee that this little activity of theirs will run, snag, and completely ruin the sheer fabric!

MEASURING

This is the same as for most of the other shade applications we have already discussed. You should be accurate within $1/8$ inch on both width and height, since the movement of the vanes tends to play a part in the overall length.

CLEANING

Silhouette is static- and dust-resistant. The manufacturer suggests using a low-suction vacuum to remove dust or to freshen up the shades. Gentle spot-cleaning with a damp sponge and mild cleanser is another option.

Luminette Privacy Sheers

This is the newest product introduced by Hunter Douglas, the people who make Silhouette. It is one of the most innovative products I have seen in a long time. It combines the beauty of a sheer fabric with the practicality and privacy of vertical blinds.

Imagine sheer pleated draperies attached to the vanes of a vertical blind. The sheers traverse for a soft filtered view and the vanes rotate for privacy. They are available in one-way draw or center-split draw styles.

Luminette privacy sheers also have an automatic vane alignment system, which means you do not have to adjust each vane every time you use them. This is an ideal product for sliding glass doors. I highly recommend it.

CONSTRUCTION

The fabric vanes are a neutral white nonwoven fiber. There is a choice of two different sheer fabrics: Angelica—a traditional smooth sheer, and Linea—a softly textured sheer. Each has twelve colors to choose from. The sheers are 100 percent polyester, which makes them durable and easy to clean.

The tracking system is specifically designed for smooth and reliable operation. The headrail is an off-white aluminum.

MOUNTING AND MEASURING

Luminette privacy sheers are installed and measured the same as most vertical blinds. They require a minimum casement depth of 1 inch. If you want to completely recess them, you will need a depth of 6¼ inches.

This product is available in widths up to 192 inches and heights up to 117 inches.

CLEANING

* Dust with a feather duster.
* For more thorough dust removal, use a hand-held vacuum with *low suction.*
* Spot clean with warm water using a blotting action. Treat stains with a commercially available clothing stain pretreatment solution.
* For light surface cleaning, professionally dry-clean.
* For deep cleaning, professional steam clean while the shades are hanging in place.

Solar Shades

This is a very popular product in the Sunbelt areas of the world. It is made of tranparent Mylar, which is very effective for blocking the sun's UV rays and glare while allowing complete viewing of the outdoors. These shades are often installed under other window treatments.

Solar shades are available in a few different color tones and strengths. If you are installing them on large expanses of glass, I recommend the industrial strength. The color of the shades will determine how much fade control is provided for your furniture. For example, amber will provide the maximum protection from the sun fading fabrics. Silver will provide a moderate control of fading, and clear UV a milder level of fading protection, approximately 50 percent of the protection offered by the amber color.

Another style provides control of heat and glare as well as fading. This uses a transparent layer of aluminum. It looks much like the Mylar material, and during the day it is completely transparent from the inside out, but privatizing from the outside in. At night, it appears silver and reflective on the inside, much like a mirror. I find this distracting, but if you have a severe sun problem, it is well worth the distraction. It is available in different, less reflective colors, each having its own value or rating of protection.

If this is a product that interests you, you will need to learn a whole new language, with terms such as *total solar energy, solar transmission, solar absorption, reflection, UV transmission,* and *shading coefficients.* Oh, I almost forgot, *solar heat gain* and *total heat gain.*

A few years ago, when solar and passive solar heating was going to save the world, I built a passive solar home. I loved it! And I did learn a lot about the above terms and the kinds of products available and necessary to fully utilize the sun's energy. Unfortunately, the "solar lifestyle" did not seem to catch on the way some thought it would. Nonetheless, if you are interested, there is a lot of good material out there for further research of your own.

CONSTRUCTION

Mechanism

Solar shades are available with two different types of mechanisms: the clutch cord and reel system and the spring roller system. The spring roller system has a maximum size of 122 inches wide by 120 inches high.

The size of the system needed depends on the size of the shade you are using. In large applications, you may choose to use an electric roller that automatically opens and closes the shade.

Fabric Application

The shade material needs to be spliced once you get to 60 inches wide or larger. It will be spliced for height as well if your shade is more than 60 inches high.

CLEANING

These are the cleaning recommendations of the manufacturer.

1. Operate the shade daily to "shake off" the dust. (Good luck! I don't know if I would consider this to be effective.)
2. Dust frequently with a feather duster or soft cloth. This is to prevent dirt buildup.
3. To remove fingerprints and most marks, use a solvent-type spot remover.
4. To remove excessive dirt, use a mild detergent with a soft cloth or sponge. But be sure to use sufficient liquid to prevent dirt deposits from scratching the shade surface. Dry the shade before rerolling.
5. Blot dry with a soft cloth and lightly polish to remove water spots.

Shopping Notes

When shopping for any hard window treatment, *always* ask if the installation is included in the price!

Do not take responsibility for measuring your own windows. If you mismeasure, you will be stuck with blinds that do not fit! The salesperson should come to your home and measure for you. That way, if there is a mistake, it is the retailer's problem and not yours.

Check the stacking dimension of any shade or blind you are purchasing. The reason this is important is that if you are using a valance or other decorative treatment over the shade or blind, you may want to hide the blind beneath. If so, you will be disappointed if your stacking space is larger or longer than the planned decorative treatment. In other words, consider every factor—you don't want your blind sticking out from under your valance!

Order all treatments for any given area at the same time. Pattern availability and dye lot matching cannot be guaranteed in the future.

Words of Wisdom

If the string operating the pulley of your shade or blind is a noose style, then please cut it into two pieces of string. Many children and pets have been fatally hung in the noose.

Vertical blinds make noise if you have them on an open window through which a breeze is blowing. The clatter can be very distracting, as I found out when I opened the verticals I have in my foyer to let in the gusty days of spring.

MORE WINDOWS—SOFT WINDOW TREATMENTS

oft window treatments generally refer to window treatments that are made out of fabric. These fabrics are purchased by the yard, as opposed to the specialized fabrics used for making pleated and honeycomb shades. And they can be one of the more expensive decorative features in a room. Because you can't sit on them, sleep on them, or drive them, most people have difficulty justifying the cost associated with draperies. They will, however, ultimately have a great impact on the overall stylish appearance of your home.

This is truly the most complex area of home fashions. There are a few basics, but only a few. There are as many different styles of soft treatments as there are people. During the seventies things were simple. Complex drapery treatments were not very popular. Now, it is amazing how many different combinations of fabric, trim, and style you can attach to one window!

Don't get me wrong—I love the opportunity this gives me for exploring my creativity, but explaining, pricing, and attempting to figure out yardage requirements nearly requires a computer and a genius.

Ultimately, your drapery treatment will be the most reflective element of style and character in your room. Your windows are the place where your room's personality will really shine. How formal, casual, opulent, or practical you really are will be expressed by your draperies.

The Basics

There are basically four different elements to any soft window treatment:

1. **Fabric**—This is the stuff of which they are made, and usually includes an exterior fabric as well as a lining fabric.
2. **Labor**—This is the cost of actually constructing your window treatment. The final price is based on time, intensity of labor, and skill of the seamstress.
3. **Hardware**—This is all the different types of hardware required for making and installing your window treatment. It includes, but is not limited to, poles, rods, finials, holdbacks, L-brackets, anchors, hooks, and rings.
4. **Installation**—This is the process of putting up your window treatment. Like labor, the cost of installation is also based on time, intensity of labor, and the skill of the mechanic. Depending on the type of window treatment chosen, the installer will also "dress" your treatment. Dressing is the final sculpting of pleats, draping of swags, stretching and smoothing the fabric—overall, making it look like what you imagined. This will make the difference between a homemade look and a handmade professional look. The more complex your window treatment, the more important this aspect becomes.

It is these four elements that will determine the cost of your window treatment. And as a result, it makes it difficult to "shop" price. In most cases, you won't really know the skill level of the people involved until it is too late. However, I will try to break down the four basics into something a little more tangible.

Fabric

There are billions of fabrics to choose from. And the price can begin as low as $1.75 and goes as high as $1,000! Because this is the one aspect of soft window treatments with the largest number of variables, this is usually the place to look first to reduce the price of a treatment. Of course, this is also the one element that is most responsible for the character or personality of your window. This can make it difficult to sacrifice either style or practicality.

Fabrics are divided into a few different categories: upholstery fabric, drapery fabric, sheers, multipurpose or crossover fabrics, and linings. The reason for this division is the difference in the hand, or feel, and weight of the fabrics.

UPHOLSTERY FABRIC

Upholstery-weight fabric is any fabric especially made for use on upholstered furniture. It is common for upholstery-weight fabrics to be coated on the reverse side with a binding solution to add stability and durability. It looks like you smeared rubber cement on the back of the fabric. *Stability* refers to how much or how little "stretch" or "give" a fabric has. *Durability* refers to the strength or ability of the fabric to wear well with use. The coating or binding product makes the fabric

ROMAN SHADE

stiffer. As a result, it is very difficult to work with and requires a heavy-duty sewing machine to process. Most drapery workrooms are not equipped with this type of sewing machine.

Uses: The best application in window treatments for upholstery-weight fabric is in "upholstered" window products such as valances, cornices, lambrequins, Roman shades, and, if you have a willing seamstress, the occasional drapery. (I'll explain what all these terms mean later.)

Upholstery-weight fabrics are usually produced in 54-inch widths.

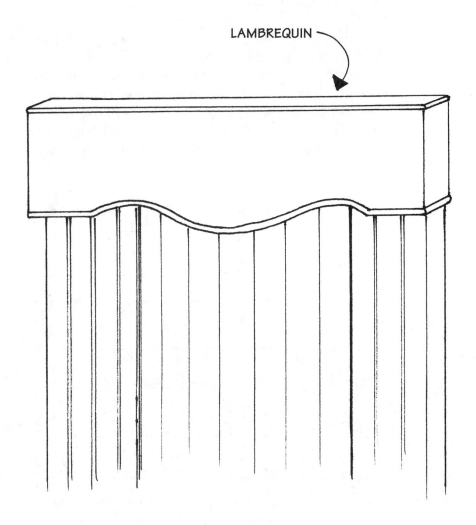

LAMBREQUIN

SHIRRED CORNICE

DRAPERY FABRIC

Drapery fabric is an all-encompassing term. It refers to the largest variety of fabrics, such as cotton prints and solids, moirés, silks, lightweight velvets, linens, and casement fabrics. Basically, it refers to any fabric with a lighter weight, making it most adaptable for draperies.

Uses: Drapery-weight fabrics can be used in almost any window treatment application. They are produced in both 48-inch and 54-inch widths.

SHEERS

Sheers are fabrics that you can see through. There are different densities or degrees of opaqueness available. Sheers also refers to lace curtains. Sheers can be made of nylon, cotton, rayon, and even silk and linen. Most often they are solid in color or have a woven pattern such as windowpane or stripe. They are often produced with a presewn hem, which is embroidered or scalloped. Some of the more contemporary manufacturers now produce printed or hand-painted sheers. These can be a bit pricey, but they are beautiful.

Uses: Sheers can be used alone or in conjunction with a more elaborate window treatment. They can be layered in various colors to create interesting cloudlike effects. They are produced in widths of 48, 54, and 118 inches. A fabric called Trafalgar Sheer or Seamless Sheers is used for the larger widths—it has specific yardage requirements, which I describe below.

MULTIPURPOSE OR CROSSOVER FABRIC

This refers to fabrics that are appropriate for either draperies or furniture upholstery. Velvets, cottons, linens, and some woven fabrics are included in this list.

Uses: The specific weight of the fabric affects the kinds of things that can be sewn with it. Multipurpose fabrics are great for tying together a look in a room. For example, using a floral cotton print on a sofa and again on the window treatment produces quite a spectacular mirrored effect. Or for a more casual or masculine look, try using a windowpane-patterned wool-blend fabric for your sofa and a matching upholstered cornice for the window. These fabrics are produced in 48- and 54-inch widths.

LININGS

Usually this refers to fabric specifically made to line draperies. This is the part you will see when you stand outside your home and look at the window. There are different kinds of lining, meant to create different effects. The basic lining is a lightweight cotton or polyester white lining. Next comes the sateen and nearly sheer linings. Then heavier, blackout (for room darkening) and extremely heavy insulating linings. It is important to choose the proper lining for your drapery fabric. Try and match like fibers—cotton with cotton, etc.—so they will react to cleaning and climate conditions in a similar manner. A word of advice: I almost never use insulating lining. It is too heavy and is not usually necessary. There are better options for insulation, such as honeycomb shades (see Chapter 7). I will not agree to draperies that are not lined, unless they are sheers. Lining is just too important to the durability and overall appearance of draperies, making them hang better, look richer, and last longer.

Fabric Yardage

How much fabric you need will obviously depend on what kind of window treatment you prefer. But there can also be a difference in yardage specified from one seamstress to the next. Why? Well, because not everyone figures as closely as the next person. Some may skimp to come in at a lower price. And in some cases, the quality of work or ultimate treatment produced can be cheap or "cheesy" looking. The technique used in the application of fabric by the seamstress will most drastically affect price and results.

I will not attempt to cover every drapery treatment known to mankind. But I will try and give you some basic information. There are hundreds of home fashion manuals available with more on this topic.

FULLNESS

Fullness is a term used to describe how much fabric is used over the width of a drapery treatment. You can choose to have $2\times$, $2^1/_2\times$, or $3\times$ the width of the overall window treatment dimension. The difference between $2\times$ fullness and $3\times$ fullness is that the $3\times$ fullness treatment will appear richer, fuller, and more elegant. Certainly, $2\times$ fullness is quite acceptable, and the cost will be less as you are using less fabric. In general, the more fabric used, the fuller the drapes will look as they hang, and for this reason I prefer to use $3\times$ fullness.

Many elements need to be considered in estimating the total yardage of your draperies. To be able to calculate this correctly, you need to factor in the measurements of the *returns*, the *overlap*, and the *side hems*. The return refers to the part of the drapery that covers the gap between the wall and the front of the drapery on either side of the treatment. This measurement is usually 3 to 4 inches for each side. The overlap refers to the amount of space that both draperies overlap when they are in the closed position. This is usually 3 to 5 inches. Finally, one should add 12 inches total (6 inches per side) to the amount of fabric needed for the finished hems on either sides of the drapery.

As an example, let's say you have a window 36 inches wide and 84 inches long, that you want to cover with a drapery with $3\times$ fullness. First, to the width, add 6 inches for the returns (3 inches on both sides), and 6 inches for overlap. This gives us a total of 48 inches. At this point in the equation, the fullness should be calculated. Multiplying 48 by 3 will give you 144 inches. You then need to add 12 inches for the side hems, resulting in a total of 156 inches. Fabrics come in a variety of widths, such as 36, 48, 54, or 108 inches. If our chosen fabric in this example is available in 48-inch width, then 3.25 widths of the fabric will be needed (156 inches divided by 48 inches equals 3.25).

Now we can calculate the length of the drapery treatment to come up with the total yardage of fabric needed. I suggest allowing 8 inches on the top and bottom for hems, which will result in a total length of 100 inches (84 inches plus 16 inches). Dividing 100 inches by 36 inches (the length of a yard) will equal approximately 2.75 lengths of fabric. This length multiplied by the width yardage (3.25) equals 8.94. Rounded up to 9, we now have the amount of fabric required for this example—9 yards.

The width of the fabric is an integral part of this equation. This is why it is necessary to know how wide a fabric is. Obviously, the larger the width of the fabric, the less yardage required.

There is one exception to this formula—*Trafalgar Sheers* or *Seamless Sheers* are figured a little differently. Because this fabric is produced in large widths (118 inches), it is meant to be turned on its side. Which means instead of running the fabric as it comes off the bolt, from top to bottom over your windows, you run it side to side. This allows for *seamless* sheers, which really improve the final appearance since seaming shows a lot on a sheer fabric. The cost per yard is more than a 48- or 54-inch wide sheer fabric. At first glance, this may seem too expensive, but in reality, you need less yardage, so the price actually evens out.

A fabric's weight also has an effect on how much "fullness" you really want. So use common sense. If a fabric is a heavyweight velvet, or has a hand-painted large-scale pattern that you want to see, then use less fullness. Under these conditions, I will concede and use a 2× (often called 2 to 1) fullness.

You would never want to use less than 3× fullness with a sheer fabric, unless it is a lace with a woven large-scale pattern that you want to expose. In this case you would allow the fabric to lay flat. Do this by using only 1 to 1 fullness.

PATTERN

This is the other major element that affects the amount of yardage required. If, for example, you chose a plaid fabric, you would have to make sure you matched or lined up not only the vertical repeat of the

A few words about color: *fabric is dyed in lots. The number of yards to a lot is determined by the dyeing technique used and the weight of the fabric. The important thing to know is that whenever you buy fabric, whether off-the-rack or by ordering from the manufacturer, you must be sure that you get all of it from the same dye lot. If it's not, there will be a difference in color from one piece of fabric to the next. There are standards that must be complied with, but what you receive may be slightly different in color from the original sample that you chose.*

pattern, but also the horizontal repeat of the pattern. In other words, you would want the horizontal lines all to be even. This means that if you have a pattern repeat of 10 inches, you must make sure you allow enough in each "cut" or width of fabric, to match this repeat. If your fabric is 54 inches wide and has a repeat of 10 inches, you will need approximately 20 percent more fabric. But each fabric pattern must be laid out individually to determine exactly how much is required.

You see how important the skill of the seamstress can be? If she is wrong on the estimate, you will be short on yardage. And it is usually next to impossible to match a dye lot, even a few days later, especially if the fabric is a popular one.

I told you this was complex!

If you are attempting to match several different fabrics for use in one space, I recommend that you call and ask for *cuttings*, or small snippets, of the current dye lots. This way you can make the decision prior to delivery as to whether or not the color is close enough for your specific situation. But be sure to reserve the necessary yardage at the manufacturer when ordering the cuttings. It will do you no good to know the color is perfect, if you find out the manufacturer is sold-out of the perfect dye lot.

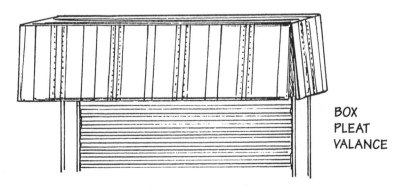

BOX
PLEAT
VALANCE

CUTTING AND YARDAGE GUIDELINE

Draperies—add 18 inches or a full repeat to finished length
Draperies—$2\frac{1}{2}\times$ minimum fullness
Sheers—$3\times$ minimum fullness
Continental rod pockets (these are 3- or 5-inch high, flat rods)—add 22 inches or a full repeat to finished length.
Regular tiebacks—7 inches for each piece
Shaped tiebacks—12 inches for each piece
Swags—2 yards for each piece
Jabots—one pair, finished length times 3 or nearest repeat
Contrast-lined jabots—one pair, finished length plus 7, multiplied by 4
Balloon shades—add 18 inches to finished length at $2\frac{1}{2}\times$ fullness
Cornice boards—finished length plus 15 inches or a full repeat
Box Pleats—$3\times$ fullness

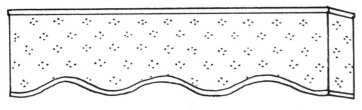

CORNICE

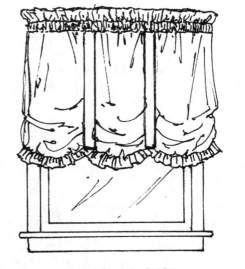

←RUFFLES

BALLOON VALANCE

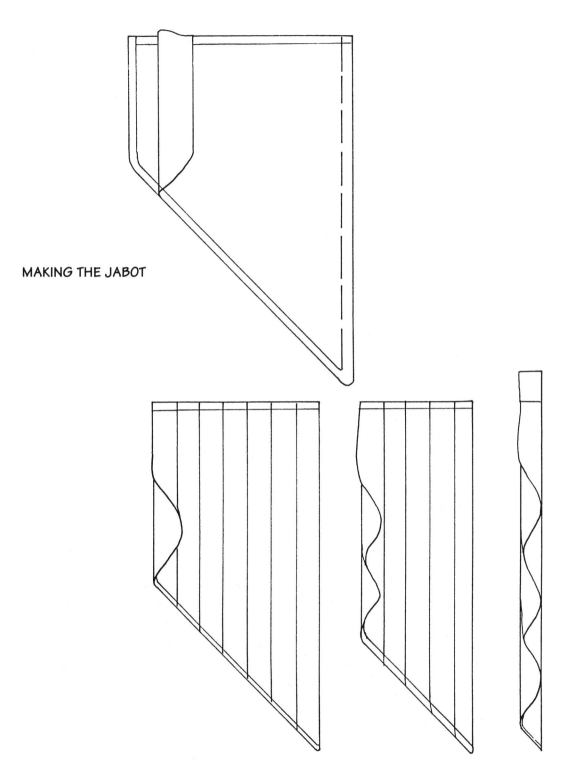

MAKING THE JABOT

Labor

At one time, this was realtively simple to figure out. But as window treatments became more complex, so has the labor associated with producing them.

Let's go back to the original example that we used to determine yardage. In that particular case, we determined that we needed 3.25 widths to get the fullness that we wanted. The labor for those draperies would be based on this same number. In other words, there is a labor price associated with each *width* required. And the amount of that labor charge will be determined by the style of draperies you request, such as pinch-pleated, rod-pocketed, tabbed, etc. (We'll discuss some of these later.)

Let's assume you want pinch-pleated draperies. The labor cost for pinch-pleated and lined draperies would be about $15 to $18/width (or panel). Therefore, $3.25 \times \$18 = \$58.50$. That would be the labor charge for your draperies. The per panel labor price will vary depending upon the style of drapery you choose.

In the case of 118-inch wide sheer fabric, the labor is based on the yardage instead of the widths. Therefore, if you need 10 yards of fabric, then you would multiply this number by the labor-related charge. Whether the 118-inch fabric is being railroaded also affects this charge.

To produce "seamless" draperies 118-inch wide fabric needs to be turned on its side. This is called railroading. However, if your ceiling is especially high, the 118-inch dimension may not be long enough to accommodate hems, headings, and the like. In that case, you would not turn the fabric on its side. You would still have the advantage of the larger width and, therefore, fewer seams.

At any rate, there is usually a difference in labor prices based on whether or not you railroad the fabric. For railroad applications, the charge is about $12/yard for pinch-pleated, unlined draperies. For 118-inch wide sheers that are not railroaded, the charge per yard is about $22. Obviously, this is to accommodate making the seams.

The important thing to remember when trying to shop price for draperies is to be sure to get a breakdown of all the different elements. There is a labor charge or fee associated with each individual piece of your window treatment.

Here is a list of some of those pieces:

One- or two-way traverse	Cornices
Pinch pleat, lined or unlined	Throw swags
Ripplefold	Roman shades
Rod pocket—top only	Smocked top
Rod pocket—top and bottom	Balloon valance
Tab curtains	Austrian shade
Diamond-shaped valances	Straight valance
Tiebacks	Sunbursts
Ruffles	Rosettes
Trims and cords	Board mounting
Shaped valances	Velcro
Rings	Buttonholes
Hinged boards	Hand-sewing trim
Grommets	Contrast lining
Swags and jabots	Box pleats
French pleat heading	

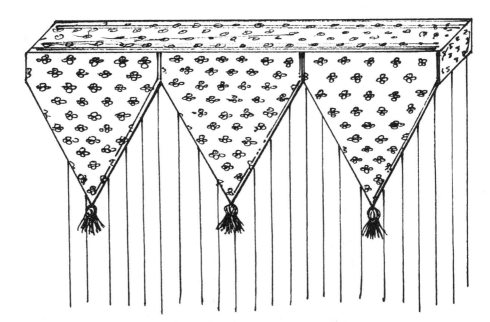

DIAMOND-SHAPED VALANCE

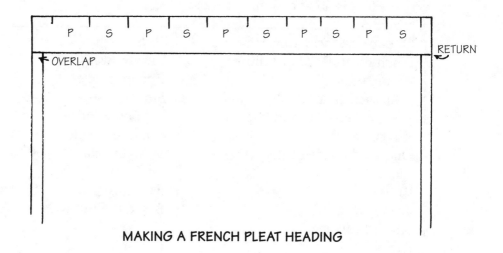

OVERLAP   RETURN

P S P S P S P S P S

MAKING A FRENCH PLEAT HEADING

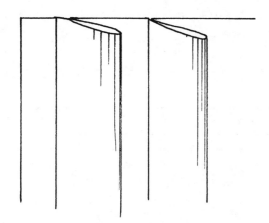
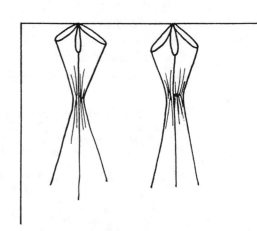

I don't expect you to know all these terms, but hopefully this will help to explain the complexity of pricing soft window treatments. Virtually every soft window treatment consists of a variety of the above components. And this is the only realistic way to compare prices.

So far, we have been discussing window treatments, but the person who sews the window treatments is also the person who will make any *bed treatments*. This includes dust ruffles, pillow shams, bed canopies, seat cushions, duvet covers (the cover for your feather comforter), and any other bed-related object you can think of!

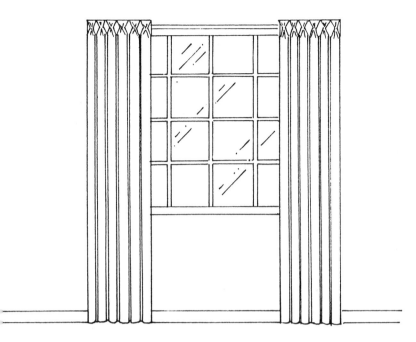

TWO-WAY TRAVERSE

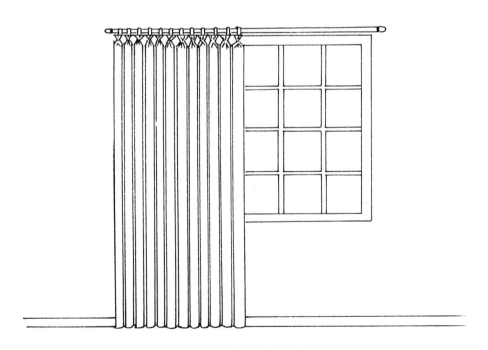

ONE-WAY TRAVERSE

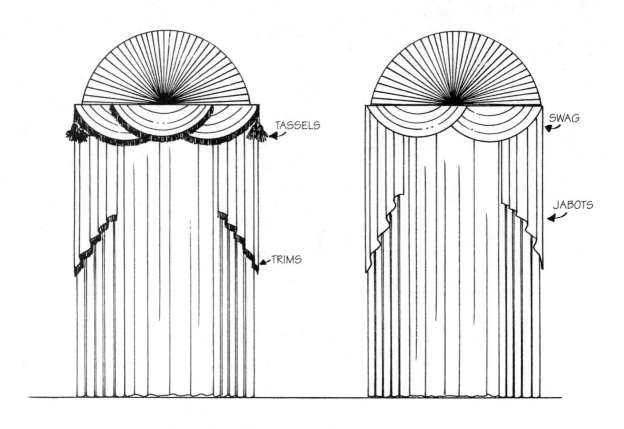

TASSELS

SWAG

TRIMS

JABOTS

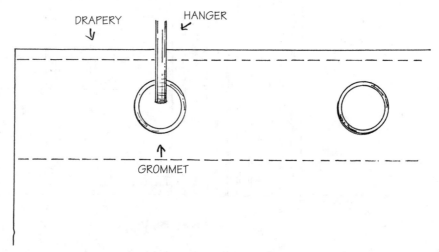

DRAPERY

HANGER

GROMMET

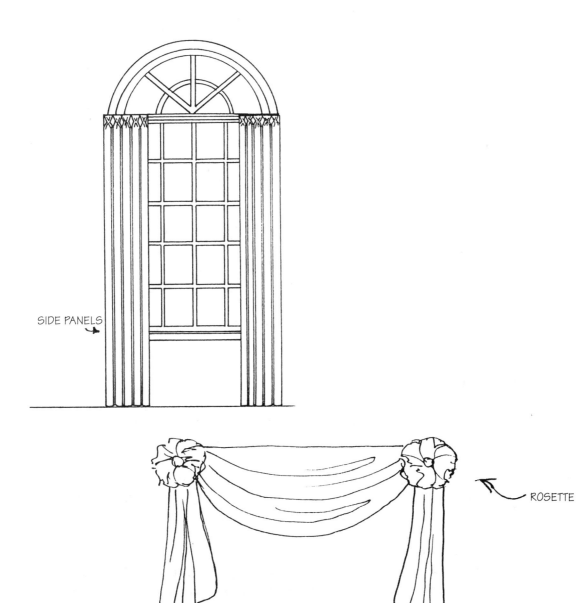

SIDE PANELS

ROSETTE

Hardware

Hardware can be even more complex than labor! In just one catalog, there can be over 100 pages of hardware for window treatments. The important thing for you to know is that there are only a few comprehensive manufacturers of drapery hardware products. This makes it relatively easy to compare pricing.

Also realize that there is almost always an alternative method for accomplishing whatever window treatment you prefer. Hardware is not the most expensive part of window treatments unless you choose decorative hardware. In that case, the sky is the limit in terms of what you can spend.

Here is what you must decide first:

❁ Do you want your draperies to move or to remain stationary? (If you choose moving draperies, then be sure to spend a little extra on drapery hardware—it's better to buy good-quality hardware now than to have to replace poorer quality hardware later on.)

❁ Do you want exposed or hidden hardware? (If you choose exposed, how important or decorative do you want it to be?)

Installation

As I said in the beginning of this chapter, the installer can make or break any window treatment.

From a practical aspect, if the hardware, blinds, valance, shades, and poles are not properly anchored to your wall, they will fall out! This is especially true of any moving element such as traversing draperies or any shade product. And that is just the beginning of what is expected from the installer.

If it is at all possible, I prefer that the seamstress install the window treatment. After all, she knows best about how the treatment is to be installed and what it should look like when finished. If the seamstress is not going to do the installation, it is often necessary to get the input of the installer before actually sewing or even measuring for a specific treatment. It is necessary that the seamstress and the installer have an ongoing working relationship. It is vital that they understand each other very well. The installer should have comprehensive notes from the seamstress and perhaps even a basic diagram of what the window treatment should look like.

After all the basics have been hung in place, the installer than should begin to hand-shape each pleat or gather in place. Often, it is necessary to "band" or tie the pleats in place with paper strips. They should remain banded for twenty-four hours to set the pleats in place.

In most cases, if the seamstress has done her job, the draperies should not need to be steamed. They should arrive already pressed. If they started out this way, a good installer will not mess them up in the process of installation.

Installation is a tedious process and requires a lot of patience and ingenuity. Often it requires working in very little space with tools that do not adapt well to those circumstances. Be patient.

Making the Right Choice

Soft window treatments are a very complex part of the home fashion industry. The people who work in this area are the real nuts and bolts of the industry.

So don't blow a gasket if everything you dreamed of didn't come true. It doesn't matter how creative, intelligent, or successful a designer is if your vision cannot be practically produced. And just like in all other professions, there is the good, the bad, and the in-between. The higher the caliber of work, the more selective most people are. This means that some seamstresses or drapery workrooms are also choosy about who they will do work for.

My own seamstress will not work with a designer who doesn't understand the mechanics of sewing and installation. I had to prove myself before she would take on any of my work. The reason is simple: if I don't understand it, I cannot possibly explain it to a client.

I am fortunate that I grew up with a sewing mother. I began sewing at seven years of age. At one time, I worked for a wonderful design firm that required each designer to actually sew a pair of draperies before they would allow us to design window treatments. They also required each designer to draw, specify all hardware, and supervise each installation that we designed. They reasoned that ultimately the designer should be responsible for all aspects of anything she designed. I probably learned more about draperies in those two years than in any time before or since.

So, as with all aspects of home fashions, it is important to interview and check out the work of anyone you are considering hiring to work in your home.

Shopping Notes and Questions

❀ Find out if all people involved have insurance, and ask to see a copy of their policy. It is important to know who's insurance will cover what if there is a problem, an accident, or damage to anyone or anything.

❀ Check out the workroom—is smoking allowed? You do not want your new draperies to start out stinking of smoke!

❀ Spend several weeks looking at magazines and catalogs for ideas before talking with a drapery retailer. Have some idea of how elaborate or simple you want your windows to be.

❀ Interview at least three different people. Do not be pushed into something you are not completely sure about.

❀ Always ask if the labor costs include ironing. You would be amazed how many workrooms do not consider this necessary. And it makes all the difference in the world to the appearance of your draperies.

❀ Be sure you are pricing "apples to apples." Get as detailed a breakdown as you can. It is the only way to know what you are getting.

❀ Find out who is responsible for inspecting the fabric. This is the person (usually the seamstress) who will look at all the fabric ordered, inch by inch, for any flaws. Flaws such as misweaves, printing problems with the pattern, slubs, snags, grease marks, or any other mark will show up in your draperies. Sometimes these flaws can be worked around and will not affect the treatment. The bottom line is, you want to know who will be responsible if a problem is not discovered until after the draperies are sewn and installed.

Words of Wisdom

Here is one way to cut cost and not sacrifice your favorite fabric. If you have chosen a style treatment that uses more than one exposed fabric, then it may be possible to use the most expensive fabric in a way that uses the least amount of yardage.

In a perfect world, the person who measures, estimates yardage, determines hardware, sews the treatment, and installs the whole thing would be one and the same. Be prepared to deal with many people, and make sure everyone is "on the same page."

Some fabrics shrink. A good seamstress will make allowance for this and be sure to make the draperies a little longer. They should then be placed a little higher on the drapery pins, so they appear to be the correct length. After they have been hanging for a season and have finished shrinking, they can be repositioned on the pins to bring them back to earth. If you are not confident about making this adjustment yourself, be aware that there will probably be a service charge when the seamstress makes a house call.

Some fabrics, such as loosely woven casement fabrics, will stretch over time. This is not due to shoddy work on anyone's part. It is the nature of the fabric. It will be necessary to have the draperies shortened later on and you will be expected to pay for this alteration. So if you are using a loosely woven fabric, ask in advance what the charge will be.

Do not "supervise" the installation, unless you are doing it yourself! If you do not trust the person doing the work, then you should have hired someone else!

Do examine any installation before the installer leaves your home. If something looks or seems odd, deal with it before he leaves. If you do not get satisfaction, call the person you ordered the draperies from before the installer leaves.

Draperies were not meant for cleaning! If it is your intention to wash or dry-clean your treatment, be sure to discuss this before selecting the fabric or style.

If you intend to take down and reinstall your own treatment, be sure it is something you can actually do yourself. If not, you will pay to have it rehung.

FABRICS, FABRICS, FABRICS!

F abric is like air for an interior designer. I cannot imagine surviving without it. Fabric affects us on so many levels. It appeals to us on a sensual, physical, emotional, and even an intellectual level. The texture, feel, color, and pattern combine to create a unique element that is the heart and soul of decorating.

We expect a lot from a piece of fabric. Not only do we expect it to meet our design requirements, but we assume it will meet our performance requirements as well. Overall, fabrics for residential use are not required to meet any legal written performance standards, unlike commercial-grade fabrics. Commercial-grade fabrics, depending on the state, must comply with fire and smoke performance levels to protect the public. And of course, there are wear and friction performance preferences for commercial-grade fabrics.

I have spent a great deal of time educating clients on what they can expect and what they should not expect from fabric. After all, fabric gets the most wear and tear when it is used on upholstered furniture, draperies, and bed coverings. Ultimately, it is the condition of the fabric that determines if something looks good, bad, or just really worn.

The most important thing to remember when choosing fabric is to match it to the task. A few manufacturers give recommendations for use, but most do not. So you must rely on the retailer or designer that you are working with to give you good advice. I love children and I believe we should allow them to *live* in a home without being cautioned on a daily basis to stay away from this or that. So I have always done my best to make family spaces durable, practical, and attractive. One way to accomplish this is to use commercial-grade products. Commercial fabrics, furniture, and office systems can easily be adapted for home use. They are usually more expensive, but they are definitely stronger because they are built to meet tougher standards than residential products. A commercial fabric can be the perfect choice for upholstered furniture in a family room. Commercial grades can be a great solution for the family that is forever replacing kitchen chairs. Explore these options when you have an application that requires the strongest products made.

Another option for increasing the durability of a fabric is to coat it. One of my clients wanted a "garden look" for her kitchen. We found the perfect wicker table and chairs. She wanted to coordinate the fabric that we used for draperies in the family room, using it on the seat cushions for the wicker chairs in the kitchen. The problem was that the fabric was very light in color and she has three children. Things were bound to get messy. The solution—vinylize the fabric. We fused a matte vinyl to the original fabric. By using a matte vinyl, we didn't change the appearance, but we now had a strong vinyl fabric that could be washed off with a sponge! It looked great and everyone was happy. This process is called *laminating*. Laminating can be used to vinylize a fabric in either matte or gloss styles. You can also laminate fabric to paper, to create a custom wallpaper. The same process can be used to create window shades, place mats, and all sorts of decorative things. Textured fabric is not a good candidate for vinylizing. The texture makes it impossible for the vinyl to get a good grip during the fusing process.

Fabrics can be treated with other products to make them stain-resistant, fire-retarding, and antimicrobial. These services are usually available through an interior designer or a higher-end retailer. Depending on the kind of product being applied, it is a good idea to order a sample of the fabric to be used as a test to be sure that there is no appreciable change in the color of the fabric. Occasionally a product can affect color and this will be a problem if you are expecting to use the same fabric elsewhere.

In Chapter 2 we discussed the basics of fabric—content, color, and construction. In this chapter, I will attempt to break down the basic fibers and their uses.

Natural Fibers

COTTON

Cotton is probably the most recognized fiber. It is the second strongest natural fabric (wool is the strongest, but cotton is more versatile and adaptable). It colors and prints well. This means that it is a good choice when you want to have several different colors in one fabric pattern. Why? Because the process of printing is done in screens. If a fabric has ten different colors in the pattern, then ten different screens need to pass over the original raw piece of goods. Some fabrics do not have the strength required to survive this process and still appear new—cotton does! Cotton is available in the largest selection of colors. It can also be woven into hundreds of different kinds of fabric such as velvet, corduroy, chintz (a smooth, highly polished fabric), denim, sailcloth, moiré (a fabric that looks as though it has been water-stained), and textured fabrics like reps or ottoman fabric (see Basic Styles of Fabric later in this chapter for a description of these).

Uses: Cotton fabric can be used for any application in window treatments, bed coverings, and upholstered furniture.

LINEN

Linen, at first glance, looks a lot like cotton. It is made from a vegetable called flax. I consider linen a luxury fabric. Why? Because only people who can afford to hire a full-time person to iron it can afford to have it! If you have ever owned a linen suit or pair of slacks, then you know what I am talking about. Oh, it has its advantages—it's pretty to look at, possesses a fine sheen or luster, and has a natural ability to resist staining. Nevertheless, keeping it from wrinkling is impossible. It also does not hold color well and will look worn long before its time. Because it is a softer, weaker fiber than cotton, it cannot take much abrasion, whether from your own hands or the printing screen. As a result, you will not find many printed linen patterns.

Uses: Linen, whether solid or printed, is a good choice for draperies, because they are generally not exposed to a lot of abrasion. But do make sure you use a quality drapery lining to protect it from fading.

SILK

Silk is one of the most expensive fabrics in the world. Why? Well, because it's made by worms! And they take a long time to produce the stuff. No matter how much you're willing to pay, you cannot speed up the process. However, the results are definitely worth it—it is one of the most exquisite fabrics in the world. It is available in two forms: raw silk and processed silk. *Raw* doesn't mean that it's just come from the worms. It means that the color is natural and so is the texture, with all of its bumps, lumps, and other little imperfections. The *processed* form of silk is shinier and has had many of the imperfections removed. Silk takes to the dyeing process in a wonderful way. Some of the richest, deepest, and most vivid hues are available in silk. Printing is not common on silk. Most silk fabrics are a solid satin style or a multitoned woven textured style. One popular process that is very effective is to hand-paint silk. On a few occasions, I have hired an artist to hand-paint a custom pattern on silk for a client. This is truly a luxury.

Uses: Silk is fairly resilient, and I have on occasion used it for upholstery. However, that is not the best application. First of all, it needs to be backed with a knit lining to make it more durable. Most often it is used for pillows or part of a drapery treatment. One example is contrast trim banding on a valance, echoed down along the side and hem edge of the draperies. It is also used to make beautiful tassels and trims. But be sure to protect it from the sun. And be aware—it will show creases if not properly ironed.

WOOL

Wool is a strong wonderful fabric. It dyes well and wears well, but it is not very adaptable. Not many people want wool draperies. First of all, they would be very heavy to traverse back and forth. Second, they would not allow any light into the room and they would make you warm just looking at them! In its defense, like linen, wool has a natural ability to resist staining.

Uses: I have made draperies of wool for a few clients. One set was for a mountain cabin. The client only used the cabin in the winter, so wool was appropriate. It is the most beautiful fabric for plaid patterns, so if used in combination with a lighter-weight fiber in a blend, it works as a heavy drapery treatment. On its own, it is great for a casual look on upholstery.

RAMIE

This not-so-well-known natural fiber comes from a plant similar to flax. Actually, it is an East Indian shrub. It is often compared to cotton because its fibers are strong, it has a nice luster and good stability, and it doesn't shrink. The bad news is that the fibers are much more brittle, which means it doesn't hold up to twisting or bending. As a result, it is rare that you will find a fabric that is 100 percent ramie.

Uses: Because it is usually blended with other fibers, it can show up in almost any configuration and, as a result it can be used for many different applications.

MOHAIR

This soft, strong, and versatile fabric is made from Angora goat hair. Popular in the thirties and forties as an upholstery fabric, it has only started reappearing in the past few years. This is probably because of the cost—it is generally a higher-priced fabric. It is the most resilient natural textile and is lightweight, crushproof, pill-proof and matte-proof. It takes color very well and holds it, resisting fading.

Uses: Most often this is an upholstery-weight fabric. But it is also used for draperies, throws, carpets, and rugs.

Synthetic/Naturals

How can something be both synthetic and natural? Well, there are a few natural products, like *wood pulp* and *cotton linters* (a by-product of manufactured cotton) that can be manipulated to create fabric fibers. So, technically, they are both natural and man-made.

ACETATE

This is a cellulose-based fabric made from wood pulp. It has a luxurious appearance and can be woven to have either a crisp or soft hand. (A "hand" is how something feels to the touch—soft, rough, light, heavy, etc.) It is naturally moth- and mildew-resistant. The best aspect of this fabric is the wide range of colors that it is available in, because it takes dyes well and prints well. The worst aspect of this fabric is that it shrinks! It reacts to changes in humidity—if you have draperies made of acetate, expect them to shrink the first summer you own them. (If you are smart, you will have your draperies made extra long to accommodate this problem.)

Uses: Acetate is most often found in drapery fabrics because of its soft hand that drapes well.

RAYON

This is also a cellulose-based fabric made from wood pulp. The basic difference between rayon and acetate is that rayon is highly absorbent and acetate is not. This means that rayon will shrink a lot more than acetate. So never, ever wash this fabric. Dry cleaning is the only recommended way to clean rayon. Like acetate, it prints and dyes well and is resistant to pilling and static.

Uses: Most often this fabric is used for bedspreads, draperies, and table linens. You will also find it blended with other fibers to create a more durable product.

Man-made Synthetics

ACRYLIC

This is made by the polymerization of acrylonitrile. Basically, this means that it is a plastic fiber. What makes acrylic unique is that it has a soft, warm, wool-like hand. The color is added while this product is still in the liquid form, which means that not only are the colors bright, but the fabric is colorfast. This also gives it a superior resistance to sunlight fading and rotting. It is resilient and resists wrinkles. But it is generally not printed, so it is limited in the styles that are available.

Uses: Most often acrylic is used for upholstery-weight fabrics, throws, and rugs.

NYLON

One of the more popular man-made fabrics, nylon is also an extruded plastic that is woven into fabric. Nylon is great because it is lightweight and strong; it also colors well and is resistant to abrasion, shrinking, and wrinkling. The problem with it is that it pills easily and cannot handle sunlight. I, for one, do not like the feel of nylon. I tend to use it more for commercial use than residential. But as a heavy-duty upholstery fabric in a family room, it can be the right choice. My biggest objection to nylon is the fact that it is shiny, a characteristic that I don't happen to find attractive.

Uses: Nylon is used for upholstery-weight fabrics and also sheer draperies. Nylon and polyester sheers are terrific. This is a perfect example of the fabric meeting the task.

POLYESTER

Polyester is yet another plastic fabric. It is very stable which means it resists stretching and shrinking. It is strong, wrinkle-resistant, abrasion-resistant, and washable. The bad news is that it stains. It also pills and can have a problem with static.

Uses: Polyester is usually found as a medium-weight fabric that is good for draperies and upholstery. However, it does not hold a pleat as a drapery. This means it will have a *billowing* effect, which may or may not appeal to you.

OLEFIN (POLYOLEFIN OR POLYPROPYLENE)

This is an oil derivative first developed in the fifties. Like acrylic, it is colored while in its liquid state. This makes it extremely colorfast. It is stain-, static-, sunlight-, and abrasion-resistant. But it really has the look and feel of plastic!

Uses: As an upholstery-weight fabric, olefin can be a good choice for heavy-duty use. It can, if necessary, be sponged clean. But it does pill.

Blended Fabrics

The majority of upholstery-weight fabrics are blended. This means that they are a combination of fibers. Blending is done for two different reasons: improving performance and creating a unique look. The competition is fierce in the home fashion industry when it comes to fabric. So creating a one-of-a-kind look guarantees attention.

By analyzing the proportions of the different fibers used, you can determine how well a fabric will perform for its chosen use. Polyester is probably the most used fiber for blending. It adds durability without completely changing the natural look of the other fibers. The more interesting the weave, texture, and highlighting a fabric has, the more fibers are used to create it.

Basic Styles of Fabric

There are hundreds of different kinds of fabric available, so I won't bore you with all of them. But I will attempt to explain the most-used styles in the home fashion industry.

Appliqué: This is the art of sewing or pasting a cutout pattern onto the surface of a fabric.

Antique satin: Satin that looks old. Actually, it is usually a satin that is not shiny, hence the antique appearance. This is usually used for draperies, pillows, and occasionally a small chair.

Batik: This employs a dyeing process called *resist dyeing.* In batik, wax is applied to create a design, then the cloth is dyed and the wax removed to reveal the pattern.

Broadcloth: Usually cotton, sometimes spun rayon. It has a small ribbed pattern in the weave.

Brocade: A woven fabric that resembles embroidery. The background is one color and the pattern is slightly raised and is usually multicolored. It can be used for draperies and upholstery.

Calico: Printed woven cotton, similar to percale. First produced in Calicut, India, hence the name.

Casement: A lightweight, open-weave fabric. This is usually made of a blend of several fibers like cotton, linen, rayon, wool, and silk. This fabric is only suitable for draperies, and it can have the problem of instability. In other words, it stretches—which means it needs to be rehemmed. You will find this fabric only in neutral shades.

Chintz: This is one of the most popular fabrics in decorating. Chintz is a printed cotton that has been glazed to give it a polished look. This also makes the fabric crisper. Because cotton prints so well, it is available in the widest variety of patterns and colors. But you cannot wash chintz, and should only dry-clean it when absolutely necessary, because the cleaning process removes the glazing.

Corduroy: A cut-pile fabric with ridges or cords. It is usually made of cotton or rayon.

Crepe: Any material with a crinkled or puckered surface. This is available in a variety of fibers such as cotton, wool, silk, or a combination of them.

Crewel: An embroidered pattern using wool yarn on unbleached cotton or linen.

Damask: A woven pattern, similar to brocade, only flatter. The pattern is created by light striking portions of the fabric's different weaves. The name has an interesting history, originating from the beautiful patterned silks woven in Damascus during the twelfth century and brought to Europe by Marco Polo.

Denim: Unless you have been in a cave for the last three hundred years, you probably know what denim is. But just for the record, it is a heavy cotton cloth—otherwise known as blue jeans!

Duck: This is a closely woven cotton fabric. Sometimes it has a plain weave and other times a ribbed weave. Similar to canvas in its feel, it is available in a striped pattern or solid.

Felt: A material that is made by matting together woolen fibers, mohair, cow hair, and other mixed fibers with heat and pressure.

Flannel: The stuff your PJs and warm winter sheets are made of. This is usually wool or cotton with a soft nap.

Gauze: This is a transparent fabric made of cotton, silk, wool, or linen. It has a rough finish.

Gingham: A lightweight cotton usually woven in checks or stripes.

Grosgrain: This is a ribbed fabric that is often used for ribbon.

Lace: At one time, this was only handmade. Fortunately, machine-made lace is now readily available. It is an openwork textile produced with needle, pin, or bobbin by the process of sewing or knitting, knotting or crocheting.

Mohair: This fabric is back in popularity, especially for blanket throws. It is a yarn cloth made from the fleece of the Angora goat. It is strong and durable.

Moiré: One of my favorite fabrics, because it is beautiful and inexpensive. It is a cotton or rayon fabric with a finish that resembles watermarks. I use it a lot for draperies, bedspreads, and pillows.

Needlepoint: A cross-stitched fabric, with a linen or canvas base.

Ottoman: A corded fabric more formal than corduroy, with a wider, flatter cord.

Rep: This is a general term for any fabric having a ribbing across the material. It is usually plain, with no pattern, and is reversible. Made of cotton, wool, silk, or synthetics.

Sailcloth: Originally the fabric used for making sails, now it refers to a heavy-duty, lighter-weight fabric.

Sateen: An imitation satin.

Satin: A basic weave fabric with a glossy finish on the front and a dull finish on the back. Originally available only in silk, it now comes in many fibers.

Shantung: A fabric that has the look of antique satin.

Swiss: A fine, sheer cotton fabric that is usually dotted.

Taffeta: Usually made of silk, it has a metallic look to its finish.

Tapestry: A heavy fabric with the pattern woven in.

Tweed: A wool fabric with a homespun look. It may be plain, twilled, or have a herringbone pattern.

Velour: Any fabric resembling velvet.

Velvet: A fabric with a short, thick pile and a plain back.

Voile: A light, transparent fabric made of cotton or wool, usually used for draperies.

Making the Right Choice

There are several areas to be concerned with when choosing fabrics: price, color, texture, durability, application, pattern, and style. Hopefully, the Ink Blot Test has helped you to find your own style and color preferences. The price you are willing to pay for fabric will be determined by your budget. Choosing the right fabric for the application will certainly make performance and durability issues manageable. Combining all of these factors is where it gets tricky.

There is an old adage that says, "The options are quality, quantity, and price. You can choose only two." In other words, it is impossible to get quality and quantity without paying the price!

I usually suggest a client start by choosing one fabric. Then begin exploring what other kinds of fabrics will work well with the original choice. It is not yet important to decide what fabric will go where. The idea is to first find out what the overall options are with any given fabric. Say you choose a floral cotton print in soft pastel colors as your first fabric. You might find that other cotton geometric patterns in the same color scheme will work well with your original choice. Stripes, checks, and plaids would also be good choices. Other options could be smaller-scale floral patterns, or mini-patterns. The key is keeping the colors the same. Adding solid velvets in two or three colors chosen from the original pattern could work well for complementary pillows. Woven cotton textures that are not too heavy would also work well. It is important not to confuse elements of style. You do not want to mix rough, heavy textures with a delicate pastel print. They just don't make the same statement.

If, on the other hand, your first fabric choice was a strongly colored geometric pattern, then you could choose heavier-textured fabric to complement it. Determining the overall character and personality of your first fabric choice will help in choosing additional fabrics for the space.

Once you have established the basic fabric choices, then you can begin to analyze the different options for their use. Usually you will find that a specific fabric can be used for a couple of different applications. The pastel floral could be used for draperies and upholstery. The same is true of the velvet or even the matching cotton mini-prints. Giving yourself these options can help keep you in budget. If your favorite fabric is also the most expensive, then be flexible in how you use it. Remember, quality, quantity, and price—choose two! Determine the application that requires the least amount of fabric and use the most expensive fabric for that application. Sometimes, by going through this little exercise, we find that another fabric may make us just as happy for less money. Most of us tend to lock ourselves into an idea; as a result, we limit our options and do nothing because we are convinced that we cannot afford to do it at all. Sometimes this may be true, but generally, there is a solution. It may require some compromise but it will still produce absolutely wonderful results.

Shopping Notes

Start a decorating file. Keep swatches, pictures, and room and window dimensions in it. Make a list of all the items you intend to purchase. Obtain and keep quotes while shopping. Being organized is not as important as knowing where all this information is kept (I keep mine in my car; that way I always have it when I need it!).

If the fabric will be gathered, pleated, or folded, you may want to consider buying *seconds* (less than perfect merchandise), which are less expensive than first-quality fabrics. When buying seconds, be sure you have purchased enough yardage for the entire project. Also be sure to visually check all the fabric before leaving the store. I know this is time-consuming, but you do not want to be surprised later to find out that a portion of the fabric cannot be used due to flaws.

Often the same fabric pattern is available from several different manufacturers at different prices. If a fabric is marked "exclusive," then it will not be available by another supplier.

Most retailers discount the cost of fabric. Be smart: always ask the suggested retail price and then ask for the discount percentage. Sometimes the retail price differs from one store to another. What really matters is the bottom line—the price you will be paying, and not necessarily the discount percentage.

Be sure to double-check the width of the fabric. If it is 48 inches wide, you will need more yardage than if it is 54 inches wide.

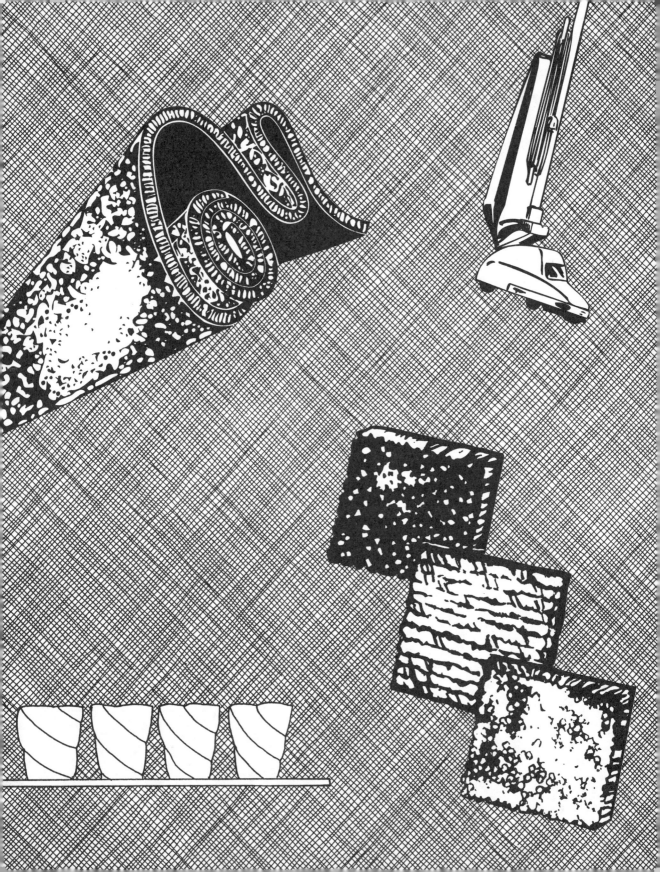

10

WHAT'S ON THE FLOOR? CARPETING!

Floors—they probably get the most abuse and the least amount of maintenance. Oh yes, occasionally we vacuum or clean, but realistically, it's usually just a "lick and a promise." It's a good thing technology has kept up with our busy lifestyles!

But no matter how progressive the technology, a little elbow grease is still the best policy.

The best bet for low-maintenance, high-durability carpets that hold their gorgeous appearance is making the right choice to begin with! So where do you begin? There are a lot of things to consider when deciding what you will cover your floors with. So, again, here come the questions:

Analyze the traffic patterns in your home:

❀ Do you use the front door, the back door, or the garage door?
❀ How do you get from the kitchen to the bedroom or family room?
❀ Do you use the patio door to get to the deck in the summer? Are you usually careful carrying ribs smothered in barbecue sauce?

Analyze your lifestyle:

❀ Do you take your shoes off the second you walk in the door?
❀ Do the kids and your husband also remove their shoes? Do they even remember to wipe their feet?

❀ Does your dog wear boots in bad weather? Probably not, so where do you clean his feet? (I use a bucket of warm water on the deck and dunk, paw at a time.)

❀ Do you have young children who will want to skate, ride, race, or jump rope on your floors? Young children also tumble and fall, and a hard surface like ceramic tile can make for a painful landing.

Special Considerations:

❀ Do you have any family members who use a wheelchair, walker, or cane?

❀ Do you have kitchen chairs with wheels? (They can really fly on a tile floor!)

❀ Do you sew or have other hobbies or crafts? Is there the possibility of losing things like pins, tiny nails, or other microscopic items? If so, you may want to consider resilient flooring or commercial carpeting.

❀ How old are your pets? The older they get, the less control they have. And cats do throw up; if they are indoor cats, they will be doing this indoors!

❀ Do you live near the beach? If so, sand is an issue. Stick with area rugs over a durable flooring.

❀ Is the soil in your area rich and red? Great for growing, but horrible for carpeting.

I could go on forever with considerations, but the point is just to get you thinking in the right direction. Obviously price, appearance, and your heart's desire have a lot to do with your final selection. And sometimes, it's best to choose something temporary until circumstances change.

Now let's examine some of the options available for finishing your floors. We'll consider carpeting in this chapter and other types of flooring in Chapter 11.

Carpeting

The basic elements to consider are:

1. **Fiber or content**
2. **Construction**
3. **Backing**
4. **Installation**
5. **Maintenance**

A combination of fiber or content, construction, and backing determines the durability and wearability of any carpet.

Fiber or Content

There are basically six different types of fiber used for carpeting: nylon, olefin, polyester, wool, acrylic, and cotton. Sometimes a combination of fibers are used (which is what the term *content* refers to).

NYLON

Nylon is the most commonly used fiber for carpeting. Most nylons used today are a fourth- or fifth-generation nylon. What does that mean? It means that technology has been able to continue to improve the configuration of the fiber to make it better in all aspects: stain-resistant, abrasion-resistant, antistatic (no more fingertip shockers!), and greater tensile strength.

Is there a difference from one brand of nylon carpet to another brand? Basically, no—as long as you stay with a brand name, such as Anso, Wear-Dated, or Stainmaster, which use nylon yarns made by major chemical companies such as Allied, Monsanto, and DuPont. Technically, the configuration of the nylon fiber is the same. What changes is what is done with the fiber. We'll discuss that later under Construction.

It gets a bit risky when you choose an unbranded nylon yarn. This usually means that a carpet manufacturer has purchased the excess nylon from one of the major production companies. They buy these yarns at a reduced price, and as a result, they are not entitled to use the company's name on their label. You get a better price, but there is no guarantee from the original producer. And you can never be sure as to what exactly you have purchased.

Colors

Each yarn type takes on color differently. Nylon is very good at accepting color. As a result, you will find a great variety of choices. However, you may not find exactly the same color in a polyester, wool, or olefin carpet. It is interesting, though, to know that different colors have different hands. Darker colors tend to be harder. This is true not only for carpeting, but also for fabrics and even crayons and colored pencils! If you like to sit or lie on the floor, you may want to try the "face test"—rubbing your face against the fibers of the carpet to see how it feels against your skin.

Warranties

Many nylon carpets carry a ten-year texture-retention, a five-year stain-resisting, and a ten-year limited resilient-wear warranty. This does *not* mean these carpets will not change in texture, or stain, or wear out. It just means they meet industry standards. The warranties vary depending on the specific brand and style. But be aware that carpet warranties cover just that—the carpet. They do not cover the labor involved in tearing out the old and installing the new!

This is where the retailer becomes very important. If you buy your carpet based only on the best price, and not on the reputation or service of the retailer, you may find out (the hard way) why there is a difference in price!

OLEFIN

This is a very interesting fiber. Basically, it's a spun plastic known as polyolefin or polypropylene. It is virtually indestructible—if used properly. Olefin should be used only to produce loop-type carpeting. I'll discuss this further in the Construction section, but basically, olefin does not do well when used as a *cut-pile* product. It gets beaten down and looks awful. The good news is that as long as you purchase loop-constructed olefin carpeting, it can last forever.

Olefin is also fade-resistant, because the color is actually poured into the plastic fiber when it is a liquid. The color goes through and through—it is not "dyed" color. Because it's plastic, olefin cannot absorb spills (technically, it has an absorption rate of 0.01 percent) and therefore is almost impossible to stain.

Years ago, I had some clients with an "alternative" lifestyle. What I mean is that they were very permissive with their children and their children's pets. They asked me to select and install carpeting for their home. Well, while I was measuring for the carpet, a dog ran through chasing a rabbit, and when I entered the living room, there was a goat! A real live billy goat! I questioned not only their sanity, but my own. What kind of carpet could I possibly suggest for this household? You guessed it—olefin—my version of spun gold. I used a Berber style (a tightly woven looped type) olefin carpet in a dirty multishaded tone of beige. It worked and it is still going strong.

So if it's so great, why is it not the only carpet on the market? Well, back to the "hand" thing. Olefin does have a harder hand—*very* hard. And because it is best used in a loop construction, it is not available or appropriate for soft, velvet-type styles. It is, however, the fastest growing carpet fiber (nylon is still the most used fiber).

Colors

You do not find the large variety of color in olefin that you do in nylon. Generally, olefin carpets are neutral shades. Occasionally you will find pastels. But for some strange reason, commercial-grade olefin carpets mostly come in a larger selection of colors such as red, blue, and green. As the demand for olefin grows, I am sure, so will the selection.

Warranties

This will vary from product to product. It will depend on the type of construction, loop or cut-pile, and the weight of yarn used.

POLYESTER

Polyester is less popular than nylon. It is also less expensive. Shouldn't that make it more popular? Well, one small problem—it's not as durable. Polyester is a softer fiber. Yes, that means it feels nicer to the touch, but it can't handle the feet! It does best in a cut-pile construction; it is also stain- and fade-resistant.

Colors

Because polyester takes on color differently than nylon, it produces different shades. So if you need a very specific color and you locate it in a polyester carpet, chances are you will not find it in a nylon carpet.

Warranties

Again, this depends on the type of construction, weight (or amount) of yarn, and manufacturer.

WOOL

Wool still holds the record for luxury. It is nature's wonder. I do not like to compare wool to nylon, because it's like comparing apples to oranges. I like them both. The texture and characteristics of wool are unique. It has a high absorption rate, so it will stain fairly easily. But it also cleans well. Personally, I have found that the lanolin in wool often chemically reacts with a stain. As a result, stains often don't look as bad as they would on nylon. Think about your favorite old wool sweater. How often do you clean it?

Wool is extremely durable. As for price, many wool carpets are now in the same price range as nylon. If you fall in love with a wonderful wool carpet—go for it!

Colors

As I mentioned, each fiber takes on color in its own way. Wool is a very absorbent fiber, so color takes and holds well. There is a huge variety of colors and textures available in wool carpets.

Warranties

This depends not only on the specific product but also on whether it is made of American or European wool. The techniques used for washing the wool is also different. I have found that New Zealand wool has more lanolin left in after washing. Some people say this is good, others say it is bad. Personally, I have had both good and bad experiences. Bottom line—know your retailer and buy only name brands you trust.

ACRYLIC

Back in the seventies this was a very popular product. But that was before technology discovered nylon. Acrylic on its own is not nearly as strong as nylon. Although the new improved acrylic is wonderful, it does have limitations. It is best suited for loop construction. This improves its strength. It is inherently stain-resistant and resembles wool in that it has a soft hand. So, if you cannot afford wool and you love the look of Berber style carpets, acrylic (trade name Acrilan) is the best choice.

Colors

Because acrylic is a soft fiber, the colors available will be similar to those of wool carpeting. They are vast, rich, and jewel-like.

Warranties

As with all the others, this depends on the specific brand and type of construction used.

COMBINATION FIBERS

A great combination is wool and acrylic. It is truly one of my favorite carpets. Usually consisting of 55 percent wool and 45 percent acrylic, this carpet is most often made in a loop-style construction. The size of the loops and thickness of the fibers will vary, creating interesting patterns and textures. This combination has terrific performance properties. It retains its shape, repels water and staining, is easy to clean, and is flame-resistant. It is also static-, fade-, and mildew-resistant. I love this carpet! Yes, it is not cheap, but it will wear well and virtually shows nothing! It is easy to maintain and pleasant to walk on.

Colors

Generally this carpet is made in neutral and natural shades. Because it is almost always a Berber style or loop construction, those are the best color choices. Most often, these carpets are variegated or tweedlike in overall appearance.

Warranties

This has a long-term warranty. Again, the length of the warranty will depend on the individual manufacturer.

OTHER FIBERS—THE NATURALS

In addition to the fibers we've discussed above, there are some wonderful, less-known and less-used fibers—cotton, sisal, sea grass, and jute. These are specialty carpets—they have a look and feel that no other fiber can duplicate. Their properties and performance are completely different as well. And as a result, you cannot compare them to the others.

Cotton

Not a lot of manufacturers produce cotton carpeting. Why? Because it is not suitable for very many places. Cotton carpet, in a cut-pile style, is soft and luxurious. It feels great to squish between your toes. It is exactly this softness that makes it perishable. I would only recommend using this beautiful carpet in places that get very little traffic and where no shoe would ever dare go. A good place would be a master bedroom suite.

Colors. So far, cotton carpet is produced mostly in natural and lighter tones. Because of its limited use, I do not expect that the selection will change much in the future.

Warranties. A good name brand manufacturer will guarantee cotton carpet against unusual wear. But accept the fact that this carpet is special and is to be used only in special areas.

Sisal (Coconut), Sea Grass, and Jute

These carpets are all very similar in quality and texture. They are wonderful natural fibers. The overall hand is also natural, which means they are firm and usually rough. But that is the beauty of these fibers. I recommend only those that have a backing applied to them. Usually this is a latex coat that provides stability and ease of installation. Most often, the carpet is cut to room size and just laid in place. There are a variety of woven textures available. The more complex the weave, the more expensive it is. I have used these natural products in all parts of the home. They are not necessarily the most comfortable carpets to walk barefoot on, but they have a great look! Because they are natural, they will absorb stains and will wear with use.

Colors. These carpets are almost always available in natural colors only. After all, whoever heard of pink grass?

Warranties. These will be based on the specific fiber and the construction of the fiber. You will not get the same kind of extended warranty with these carpets as you would with the more traditional fiber carpets.

Construction

The easiest way to discuss construction is to define basic terms. It is a combination of these terms or techniques that will determine the construction and resulting durability and performance of your carpet. So, here goes.

CONTINUOUS FILAMENT

This generally refers to nylon fiber and is exactly what it sounds like—one continuous piece of nylon that is woven into a backing to create a carpet. The advantage of this type of construction is that because it is one continuous piece of fiber, there is less pilling and less fuzzing. There is also less breaking of the fiber. But this construction may not be suitable for a style that requires shorter lengths.

CUT STAPLES

The opposite of continuous filament—the strand is actually made of many shorter strands twisted together. The problem is that it will pill, shed, and fuzz when rubbed. But sometimes it is the only thing that will work to produce a specific look you are trying to create.

CUT PILE OR PLUSH

This technique uses level-cut fibers to create the carpet. The denser the carpet (the more strands per inch), the plusher it is. Pile height will vary as well.

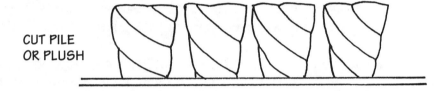

CUT PILE
OR PLUSH

DENSITY

This refers to how tightly the fiber is stitched into the backing. Obviously, the tighter it is, the more resistant it is to crushing or matting. Why? Because the tighter the fibers are, the more yarn is used. Imagine yarn fibers standing $1/2$ inch away from each other. See how easily they can be crushed down into the vacant space next to them? Now imagine the fibers packed tightly together, with virtually no space between. It would be very difficult to crush or matte them down because there is no place for them to fall.

DURABILITY RATING

This is a "walk test." The industry standard is twenty thousand steps! The results are based on appearance, shedding, crushing, and matting after twenty thousand steps. The ratings are from 1.1 to 1.4. The higher the number the better.

TEXTURED OR TRACK-FREE

This is usually a cut-pile carpet that has twisted tufts that hide footprints and vacuum marks. Sometimes this will be a combination of cut pile and loops to create even more texture.

FACE WEIGHT

This refers to the number of ounces of fiber per square yard. The more yarn, the tighter the density and the greater the durability. It also means the higher the face weight, the more expensive the carpet.

LOOP

Just like it sounds, the carpet consists of loops of fiber, sometimes referred to as a Berber style carpet. They can be level loops, or multi-level loops.

COMBINATION CUT AND LOOP PILE

TWIST

This refers to the number of times a fiber is twisted in a 1-inch length. The more times it's twisted, the more resistant it is to crushing and the better its long-term appearance.

STENCILED CARPET

There are basically two ways to create a patterned carpet—weave the pattern into the carpet or print it on top. Stenciled carpet is exactly what it sounds like—a pattern is printed on top of the carpet. This is a less expensive process than weaving the pattern in. You get a better price, but in heavy-traffic areas, the pattern can wear off!

WOVEN PATTERN

The pattern or design is woven into the carpet. In other words, a computer is programmed to actually weave a specific pattern. This is obviously more expensive than stenciling, but the pattern is through-out the entire carpet and not just on the face of it. This technique is usually used on very expensive and commercial carpeting.

COMMERCIAL CARPETING

Basically, commercial carpeting has more yarn per yard and a much shorter pile height. As a result, it is much more durable. I often use commercial-grade carpeting in basements and home offices, and even in family rooms. I figure if it can hold up to the wear and tear that commercial installations experience, it might be able to handle the abuse a family can give out!

Backing

This is what holds your carpet together. It is also what will stabilize your carpet, keeping it from stretching.

The standard backing is what's called 5 or 6 pick-back and is usually made of polypropylene. A more expensive carpet may have an 11 pick-back. This means the weave is closer together, making for a heavier, tighter type of construction.

Ninety-five percent of carpets are tufted through the primary backing only. Only 5 percent use an interlock weave, which goes through primary and secondary backing. This is much like the technique we used to make potholders as kids.

Some wool carpets use a *jute* backing. Because jute is a natural product, it makes sense to use it with wool, another natural fiber. It works well and looks great. Jute is strong, durable, and resilient. However, it may mildew in damp conditions.

Installation

Installation is another one of those areas where the person actually doing the work can make or break the job. It makes me crazy when people make their decision on where to purchase based simply on price. Installation prices can vary a lot. Why? Because the quality of the work can vary a lot! And unfortunately, you often cannot control who will be installing your carpet. Why? Because many of the installers are independent contractors. Therefore, the retailer may hire a variety of independent contractors and simply hand out work as it comes in. Yes, they certainly would not continue to use a contractor they have had problems with. But they do not have control over who the independent contractor hires! So again, the reputation of the retailer is very important. Ultimately, this is the person you will be expecting to warrant and service your products!

Sometimes it is necessary for the installer to come back and restretch your carpet. This does not mean the original work was defective. It is expected with certain carpets, especially heavy or stiff ones.

The temperature of a room can affect the installation. If a room has not been kept at least 68 degrees for a twenty-four-hour period, it can make it nearly impossible to properly stretch the carpet into place. This is a common problem with new construction.

TACKLESS INSTALLATION

This is the most commonly used method of installation. It is called *tackless* because it uses wood strips with little nails that are bent slightly to grab the carpet and keep it in place. The old-fashioned way used carpet tacks that were pounded through the carpet to the floor to keep it in place.

GLUED-DOWN INSTALLATION

This is exactly as it sounds. The carpet is directly glued down to your floor. This type of installation is usually used only on concrete floors. And, as a result, it is most often used in *commercial* installations.

Generally, no padding is used with this method. However, some commercial-grade carpets specifically designed to be glued down now have a pad already attached. There are also pads made for this purpose. They are first glued to the floor and then the carpet is glued to the padding. This is an excellent method of installation for a finished basement area. But be aware that when the time comes to install new carpeting, the removal process is very time consuming, and you will pay for it!

PADDING

This is the foundation for your carpet. There are many, many different carpet pads on the market, so choosing the right one can be confusing. Basically, the density is the most important aspect of padding. The denser the pad, the more support it will give your carpet. A density between 6 and 8 pounds/square yard is a good choice. Certain carpet types have a manufacturer-recommended type of padding. Pay attention to this—it will affect your warranty.

Most people think that thicker is better. Not necessarily. The thicker the pad, the more difficult it is to walk on, especially in high heels! The industry standard is a pad $1/2$ inch thick consisting of either a prime urethane or a rebond pad. The prime urethane has more air and therefore feels softer. The rebond is denser and firmer. Some say rebond is better, but I think it is a matter of preference. Do not use a cheap pad. I would rather you spend a little more, even with cheaper carpeting. It will lengthen the life of your carpet.

Some carpet pads are now treated with an antibacterial product. This originally was designed for use in health care facilities, but I think you will see this become more widely used as time goes on.

YARDAGE

Why is it one person says you need 28 yards and the next says 31 yards? It all has to do with where they put the seams. There is always, or almost always, more than one way to lay out a carpet installation plan. It's easy if your room is less than 12 feet wide, because most carpets are produced in 12-foot lengths. But things get a bit more complex when your room is larger.

It's ideal if seaming can be avoided in the most trafficked areas. And it's also nice if seaming can be avoided in the middle of the room. Sometimes this is not possible, but it is what we strive for. So, based on where you want seams, the yardage may change.

Another factor is that all the carpeting should be running in the same direction. Imagine the carpet as it is being pulled off the roll. Well, no matter where or how you cut and seam it, the direction of the fiber should remain the same. If it gets turned, the color will appear different. Sometimes, to save yardage, an installer will quarter-turn a piece. Yes, it saves on yardage, but it also changes the color. I *never* recommend this.

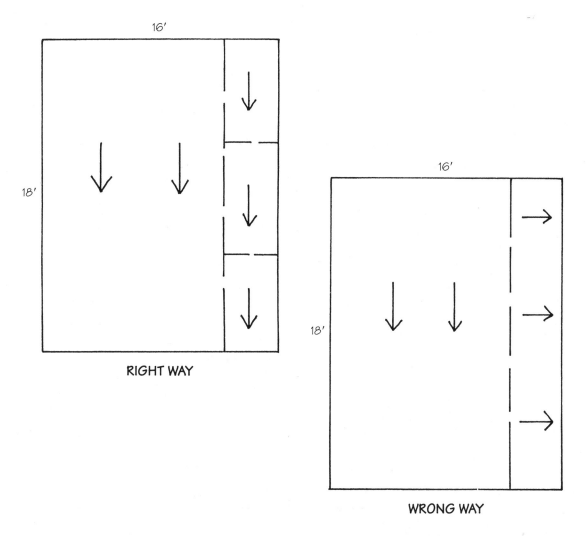

RIGHT WAY

WRONG WAY

TIPS FOR INSTALLATION DAY

You also have some work to do when your carpet is being installed.

1. Vacuum the old carpet before the installer arrives.
2. Before installation begins, inspect the new carpet for proper color, style, and visible defects. (The installer wasn't there when you chose your carpet, so he has no idea what color it should be!)
3. Open a few windows or doors for ventilation during installation.
4. Vacuum the floor under the old carpet when it is removed.
5. After the installer leaves, vacuum your new carpet, even if the installer has already done so.
6. The installer will often take down your doors in order to install your carpet. However, it is *not* his job to trim your doors if they now stick because the new carpet is higher than the old. This is your responsibility.

Here are some things to expect after your carpet is installed:

1. There will be a lingering odor that will dissipate in a few days. Ventilate the room as much as possible until the odor is gone. If you are extremely sensitive, then plan to stay somewhere else for a few days.
2. You will experience some shedding of the carpet for a few months. These are just fibers that have loosened when the carpet was cut and milled.
3. Sprouting. No, it's not growing! This happens at the seams and along the walls when longer fibers stick up where the carpet has been cut. Just clip these longer fibers with scissors.
4. The color seems to be changing! Yes, as the carpet gets walked on, the angle of the fibers may change, and hence the color may appear different.
5. After a few months, you may see some buckling and wrinkling. This does not happen often, but if it does happen—don't panic. Call your retailer and ask to have the carpet restretched. There is not usually a charge for this.

Maintenance

The three most important things to know about maintenance can be summed up simply—vacuum, vacuum, vacuum! And run as fast as you can for paper towels when something gets spilled!

Okay, now that I've made my point, I'll be a little more detailed.

The Carpet & Rug Institute recommends vacuuming heavily trafficked areas *daily*. They recommend you use a good vacuum, which is one having either a very strong single motor or two motors, with powerful airflow, high-efficiency filtration, and an internally housed vacuum bag. (Whew!) They also recommend that you properly adjust the height of your vacuum to meet the specifications of your carpet. In other words, follow my first instructions!

Stain-resistant does not mean a carpet will not stain. It simply means that the more resistant to staining it is, the more time you have to run to get the paper towels before whatever was spilled actually penetrates the protectant and begins to stain the carpet. *Always* keep a roll of white paper towels in the house just for this purpose. And do not rub the spill or stain. Blot, blot, and blot some more. Once you have blotted as much as possible, then find the manufacturer's original directions for dealing with stains. If you cannot find this elusive piece of paper, get the 800 number from the directory and call ASAP! If you do not follow the manufacturer's recommendation, then they do not have to honor any warranties.

There is a phenomenon known as "recurring stains." What this means is that no matter how good a job you or a professional do on cleaning a stain, sometimes it comes back. And sometimes, it keeps coming back, bigger and darker than ever before! This is no one's fault. It has to do with the specific chemical makeup of both the carpet and the stain. No one can predict when this will happen, it just does.

Recognize that it is a fact and don't panic. My best advice is not to wet the spot too much. The deeper you dampen, the more likely you are to make the stain permanent. It is best to let professionals deal with this monster. Sometimes, if they can guess at the chemistry involved, they can come up with a solution that works. If not, you will just have to keep recleaning the spot!

Long-term care for your carpet is defined by most manufacturers as *deep cleaning* every twelve to eighteen months. I hesitate to tell you exactly what they mean by this. I would suggest you call the retailer and/ or manufacturer and get their exact opinion.

Shopping Notes

Always ask to see the *seam plan* for your home. Be sure you are happy with the placement before ordering the carpet! Check to be sure the direction of the nap is consistent throughout.

It is not the installer's job to move your furniture. They may do it, but it will cost you.

If you have a china cabinet or any other cabinet filled with precious artifacts, please, *please* remove them before the installer arrives.

If you want your old carpet removed, there will be a charge. If you want your old carpet disposed of, there will be yet another charge.

Always take samples home to view. Fluorescent lighting (which is found in most stores) will change the color of the carpet. Look at the carpet both during the day under natural light and at night with incandescent lighting.

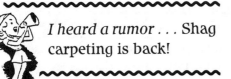

I heard a rumor . . . Shag carpeting is back!

The Indoor Air Quality Consumer Information Board recommends ventilating any new carpet for seventy-two hours. Some people, especially infants, can have an extreme reaction to the odor and chemicals of new carpeting. I have a niece who had to be hospitalized because of this. So if you have any concerns, take precautions and make arrangements to stay elsewhere for a few days.

You can call the Carpet & Rug Institute at 800-882-8846 if you have questions about indoor air quality.

Words of Wisdom

When working with clients, I often tell them, "There is no such thing as the 'perfect' house." Keep this in mind—a house, like people, constantly changes.

If you are planning on building a new home, shop for carpeting before pricing construction costs. Why? Because many builders use unreasonable budgets for carpeting and flooring to reduce the overall price. If you know the real cost before shopping for a builder, you can use real numbers rather than "budget" numbers for pricing.

Accept the fact that nothing is forever, and that includes carpeting.

A carpet that looks "dirty" to begin with will not show the real dirt, when it inevitably shows up!

11

WHAT'S ON THE FLOOR?
WOOD, TILE, STONE,
VINYL, AND LAMINATE!

If you're reading this chapter, it means you probably have decided you want to use something other than carpeting on your floors. But what?

The biggest problem with the home fashion industry is that there are probably too many options. It's overwhelming, even for me, and I live, breathe, and sleep this business. I can only imagine how you must feel.

Hopefully, I can help shed a little light on the subject.

Wood Flooring

PREFINISHED WOOD FLOORING

I guess I'm a little more old-fashioned than I thought. It took me a long time to warm up to *prefinished* wood flooring. Why? Well, I had some problems with the original finishes. They scratched too easily and required special care. They also often had *grooves* or *v-ridges* between the planks, which were great dirt collectors. Okay, so maybe I'm picky. But as technology has improved, so has my opinion of prefinished flooring.

Just as with all other products, there are a variety of prices and qualities to choose from. And yes, some of them still have those dreaded grooves and rotten finishes. But there are a lot of good products available now as well.

Pricing

The first thing you need to understand is pricing. The published or listed price for wood flooring usually refers to price per square foot. To do a price comparison of wood flooring versus carpeting, you would need to multiply by nine (the number of square feet per square yard) to make it a comparable price structure. So if the wood floor costs $7/square foot, it would cost $63/square yard.

The price range for prefinished wood flooring is $6.50/square foot to $10/square foot installed. Obviously, if you start to get fancy with borders and all sorts of inlays (patterns), your price will be higher.

You will find that prices will be lower if you purchase through a stocking dealer. Why? Because they get better pricing since they buy in larger quantities.

The basic factors affecting price are:

- ❀ Thickness of product
- ❀ Types of wood choices available
- ❀ Style, such as planks versus parquet
- ❀ Finishes

Finishes

Urethane. Almost all prefinished floors use a urethane finish. The difference in durability and appearance will be dependent on how many coats of urethane were applied. The average midrange product should have seven coats of urethane.

You can choose between gloss and matte finishes. This is really just a matter of personal taste. I prefer a matte finish. Somehow, the gloss just looks too much like plastic to me.

Acrylic Impregnated. This is actually more than a finish. The wood is literally injected with acrylic. The acrylic gets into the pores and nooks and crannies of the wood to create an incredible product. It still looks like wood but performs like steel.

You will pay more for this product, but it is well worth it for heavy-traffic areas.

Stain Colors. Again, this will depend on the individual manufacturer. But do not expect to be able to customize your color. If you want something really out of the ordinary, then use an unfinished floor, have it custom colored, prefinished, and then installed. You will get all the advantages of a prefinished floor along with the custom options of an unfinished floor.

Styles

There are many options when it comes to choosing a pattern or style for your wood floor. And the options will vary from one manufacturer to another. Here is a list of some of the basic choices:

- Parquet—a pattern created with short blocks or pieces of wood
- Random-width planks—some of the planks will be narrow and others wider
- Chevron—a pattern sort of like a lot of V's lined up in a row
- Regular-width planks—just like it sounds
- Bordering
- Specialty designs—such as a starburst in the center of your room
- Wood choices—some of the more interesting woods are red oak, birch, maple, and cherry

Installation

Usually the advertised price includes installation, but not always. So be sure to ask. Also ask if it includes subflooring. And if so, what kind?

Here comes my lecture again: the reputation of the retailer is directly related to the quality of the installation you will receive! All warranties and service-related issues will be the direct responsibility of the retailer. Know and like your retailer or do *not* purchase from him!

At one time, glued-down installations were the best option. But

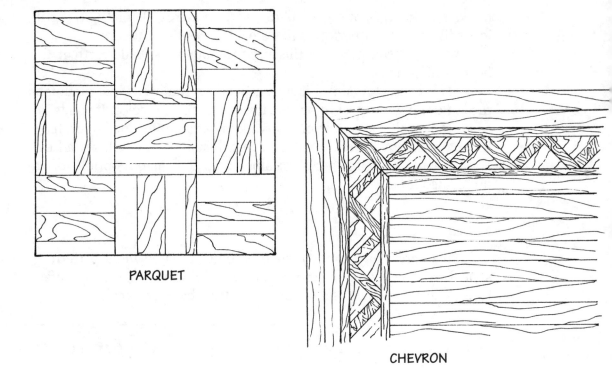

PARQUET

CHEVRON

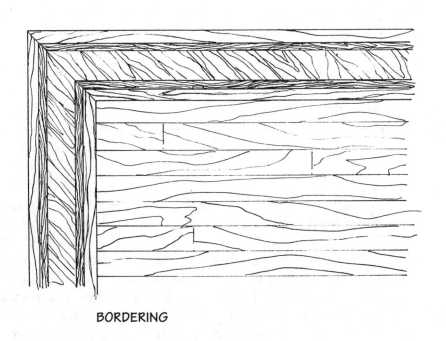

BORDERING

this is not so anymore. The reason is that due to environmental concerns, the chemical makeup of the adhesives has been changed. And quite frankly, they do not stick as well as they used to.

As a result, the most popular method of installation today is nailing, or tongue and groove with or without an adhesive. Tongue and groove means that each board has one side with a groove and one side with a tongue (similar to a dovetail method) which hook together.

As with all things, a strong foundation is important. Preferred subflooring is plywood. I prefer this to wafer board, because wafer board is more absorbent and therefore acts like a wick in damp situations. Of course, there are different qualities of both types, and as always, you get what you pay for.

Actually, all wood reacts to extreme temperature and climate changes. So no matter what kind of wood floor you choose, there will be some expansion and contraction. As a result, it is necessary to allow room for this during the installation process. This is done with new construction during winter. If it is unusually cold in the house when the floor is being installed, the installer will have to leave some expansion room between the floor and the wall.

Another consideration with wood flooring and installation is if you have a wood stove. Wood stoves have the ability to pull every ounce of moisture out of a floor, and as a result, your floor will shrink! And if the floor is in a basement, or a room built on a slab, and there is a dampness or moisture problem, this will only compound the problem. You will have a mess on your hands. And it will not be the fault of the installer.

Advantages of Prefinished Flooring

Unfinished flooring, after it is installed, has to be sanded. And it is virtually impossible to get any electric sander all the way up to the edge of the wall. As a result, there will always be a slight sanding mark left behind.

With a prefinished floor, you know exactly what the color will be *before* it's installed.

Very few unfinished floors get seven coats of urethane.

With a prefinished floor, all the ugly and bad boards are certain to have been discarded before finishing.

It is actually less costly to do creative patterns with prefinished flooring than it is with unfinished flooring.

UNFINISHED WOOD FLOORING

This is much more difficult to be specific about. Why? Because we're not working with specific brands or manufacturers. There is an unlimited pool of suppliers and mechanics. And as a result, the price, quality, and workmanship will vary far too much to realistically discuss here. But basically, expect the price range to be very similar to that of prefinished flooring.

Personally, I still believe unfinished wood flooring has a place. I built a new home a few years ago and had an old-fashioned floor mechanic put in a beautiful oak floor in my dining room and foyer.

Finishes

Well, that depends on what you want.

The basic two options are durawax and urethane (matte or polished). Each has its own characteristics and maintenance issues.

Installation

A tongue-and-groove type installation is almost always used for unfinished wood flooring.

Advantages of Unfinished Wood Flooring

The most important advantage is the ability to customize the color. Recently I had a beautiful white oak floor stained a soft peachy-rose color. I then had it washed in an off-white. To add a custom detail, we added hand-painted accent borders. Finally, we applied several coats of urethane sealer.

We were able to control the color and patterning of floor. This kind of work cannot be done with a prefinished floor.

ANTIQUE WOOD FLOORING

This idea comes and goes, and currently it is popular again. I've always liked it. Basically, you purchase flooring from the deconstruction of an old home or barn. That flooring is then stripped of nails and the old finish is removed. The floor is then installed and a new finish is applied.

You end up with a really wonderful effect. It has the richness of the wood with the added warmth of the aging of time. It can work well in both traditional and contemporary styles. Here in Lancaster County, Pennsylvania, the Amish are great at taking apart aged structures and reusing most of the old parts for new buildings. The use of old floors is always a popular idea here.

A funny aside: years ago, a client of mine bought an old home. He had actually purchased it more for the land than for the home itself. He planned to demolish the home and build a new one on the old foundation. So he hired several Amish men to come and demolish the old house. There was also an old barn on the property. In passing, he mentioned to one of the Amish that some day he would have to do something with the old barn. Well, the Amish man misunderstood my client's comment. When my client returned the next day, the barn was gone too!

Laminate Flooring

Okay, you want the look of wood, but the durability of iron. How can you accomplish this? Easy: *laminate flooring*.

This is the latest and the greatest to hit the market! Basically, it is the same stuff they make kitchen countertops from. Yes, like Formica brand laminate. And this same kind of durability and ease of maintenance is now available for your floor!

This product is guaranteed not to stain, wear, or fade for ten years!

Disadvantages

Laminate flooring can be used almost anywhere. I did say *almost* anywhere. There is only one place that I do not recommend using this product, and that is in wet areas. Why? Because the base or foundation of this product is wood. And it will absorb the moisture and warp, warp, warp! So do *not* use it in a bathroom.

Currently laminate makes up about 7 to 12 percent of the flooring market. But I think it will become far more popular in the next few years.

There is only one other small disadvantage and that is that it tends to sound hollow. This is because it is a "floating" floor. The laminate itself and the tongue-and-groove installation technique give it its hollow sound. One manufacturer, Armstrong, has found a solution to this problem. They have added an acoustical barrier to their subflooring. This is a rolled-foam layer, and it really does help reduce the hollow sound.

All of these products are manufactured in Europe. Pergo brand, made in Sweden, has the overall best foundation.

Pricing

Obviously, if you get really creative (and you can with this product), it will cost more. But a general rule of thumb is to expect to pay $7 to $8/square foot. Installed.

Construction

There are basically three components to laminate flooring.

Surface. This is a durable, water- and wear-resistant floor laminate (high-pressure melamine laminate) that is bonded to a core. This product is actually about twenty times more resistant than the material used for countertops.

Wood-Based Core. They say this is moisture-resistant. But remember, we are talking about wood—how resistant to moisture can it really be? The core is then bonded or glued to a balancing layer.

Balancing Layer. This is what gives the product stability.

Installation

As I said earlier, this is a tongue-and-groove installation technique. And if you are a really good do-it-yourselfer, you can certainly install this floor yourself.

Styles

This product has an amazing number of options when it comes to patterns and styles. One manufacturer offers thirty-two different patterns to choose from. And I expect that as its popularity grows, so too will the number of options.

The majority of patterns are woodlike in appearance. A few others are marblelike or granitelike in appearance.

Maintenance

This is the best thing about this floor: just vacuum. If you think it really needs it, occasionally damp mop it. That's all there is to it, unless you have a specific stain or situation. Then, refer to the manufacturer's suggested techniques. For example, with grease, chocolate, juice, or wine, use warm water and a mild detergent. With crayon, lipstick, shoe polish, or ink, use mineral spirits or denatured alcohol.

This stuff is guaranteed not to dent, scratch, or even be affected by a burning cigarette! What more can I say?

Resilient Flooring

Resilient flooring (usually referred to as vinyl flooring) has really changed over the last several years. At one time, people chose resilient flooring because it was basically all they could afford. In most cases, they would have preferred ceramic tile or even a wood floor. But today, things are different. Resilient flooring is now in a price range very similar to other types of flooring, such as ceramic tile, wood, carpeting, and stone products ($15 to $40/square yard). So if you choose resilient flooring it should be because of its performance properties and its look, and not because it's the cheapest thing available. (Yes, I am sure you can still find some closeouts for $7/square yard—but that's not comparing apples to apples!)

There are basically three levels or generations of resilient flooring on the market today. So I will discuss construction, installation, etc., for each of these three levels.

LEVEL ONE

Level one is the least expensive level. This product was a major breakthrough when it first hit the market, because it required no wax! And we all celebrated. At the time this was the cutting edge in technology.

Construction

The pattern is printed on a paperlike layer and applied to a felt backing. It is then sealed with either a vinyl layer or a urethane layer. The vinyl-coated floor is usually warranted for three years. The urethane-coated floor usually carries a five-year warranty.

This product is usually produced in both 6- and 12-foot widths. So if you are using it in a small bathroom, you certainly want to purchase it in 6-foot widths, to reduce the amount of waste material.

Disadvantages

The problem with this floor is that because of the felt backing, it has a tendency to mark easily. This means if you walk across it wearing women's heels, it will leave indentations across the floor.

The urethane finish used on this level of flooring is a first-generation urethane. This generation is, for the most part, pretty soft. And as a result, it is porous, which means that it will stain. That is probably the biggest complaint against urethane finishes. I am sure you have seen that yellowed vinyl floor. Or worse yet, the awful stain caused by spilled grape juice!

Because the pattern is just printed on a layer of the floor, if you do tear the floor, you will be left with a gaping white hole!

So why would anyone buy this stuff? Because it is the least expensive. And for the price, it is a great product, and therefore, a great value. You just have to be aware of its limitations and take the necessary precautions.

Installation

The subflooring is the foundation of your floor. And if it's not good, neither will your floor be. Recognize that you will pay the same price for the labor portion of your installation regardless of whether you purchase good or bad subflooring. It is definitely worth spending a dollar or more per square yard for better subflooring. Most manufacturers recommend ³/₄-inch subflooring. And be sure that the nails are underlayment nails and that they are countersunk just below the surface. You do not want the nails popping through your floor.

It is not always necessary to replace subflooring. But if you choose not to replace it, then be sure it is still securely fastened in place. Nail up any loose spots.

If you are installing over an old floor, be sure the old one is still secure. Also, remove any old wax or soap residues from the old floor before installing the new one. Sometimes there can be a chemical reaction between old floor products and the new floor. Also be aware that if your old floor is really textured, then it is necessary to add a new layer of subflooring. If you don't, you will end up being able to see the pattern of the old floor coming up through the new one!

Concrete actually works well as a base or foundation for resilient flooring. So it is a good choice in basements. The resilient floor itself will actually do fairly well, even in a damp basement. However, it may not adhere in extreme cases.

LEVEL TWO

Okay, they realized the problem of staining with level-one urethane. So they went back to the chemistry lab and created urethane two! Urethane two is harder, which means that it is less absorbent and therefore is very resistant to staining. Yeah! *But*—and you knew there would be a *but*—because the urethane is harder, it now becomes too brittle. This means that if you drop a can on it, it will leave a mark. We knew that the old urethane dented to an extent, but this new stuff *really* dents!

So to camouflage this problem, the manufacturers added more dents! In other words, this flooring comes predented, to hide any new marks you might make. And to an extent, it works. But the reality is, it's just hiding them.

Advantages

The good news is that because it still is a better product than the old urethane, the manufacturers can offer a ten-year warranty.

Construction

The basic product is the same, with a felt back. However, this generation of flooring actually has two different techniques for creating the patterns on the floors: printing and inlaying.

Printed Patterns: This is the same technique used in level one; the flooring is available in both 6- and 12-foot widths.

Inlaid Patterns: This is a very unique process. And actually, only one manufacturer, Armstrong, uses this process and it is patented by them. Inlaid means that tiny color granules are layered and then bonded (or melted) together. This creates a pattern of color throughout rather than just a thin printed layer. The advantage of this process is that the color goes all the way through—if you happen to tear or cut the floor, you won't be left with a white spot. In addition, the pattern has a richer, deeper, different kind of look. Because this product weighs more than a printed floor, it is available only in 6-foot widths. Another reason it is available only in 6-foot widths is because that is the standard size the machines were designed to produce.

Installation

The installation for this flooring is pretty much the same as for the first-level floor. But some floors in this generation need only to be glued around the perimeter, so they are a lot easier to install. These are a good choice for do-it-yourselfers.

LEVEL THREE

Now this gets exciting! Why? Well, for a couple of different reasons. First of all, the chemists finally got it right. Second, level three is a completely different *style* of product.

Construction

This third generation of urethane is "just right!"—like in the story of the Three Bears (I couldn't resist). Seriously, this urethane finish resists both staining and denting. It will stand up to the "dropped-can test"! It is also much more forgiving. Part of the reason for the additional dent-resistance is a revolutionary new backing of *glass fiber* (the trade name is Advantex). And the really good news is that not only is this floor stain-resistant, but the dirt literally floats on top of it. Even tough stains like black heel marks come right off with just the rubbing of your finger!

This floor is available in both printed and inlaid color patterns. As a result, the width will be determined by which pattern and style you choose. This product carries a ten-year wear warranty.

Style

Currently, only Armstrong has this new product and it is called Vios. What makes this product really exciting for me is the ability it gives you to really customize your floor. Up until this product was invented, resilient flooring usually tried to imitate things like stone, brick, tile, and the like. But Vios is unique. It consists of colors that are made from distinctive textures and subtle patterns. They are meant to be used together, creating borders, inlays, and patterns—even using the floor to designate spaces within a room.

One of the reasons many people object to resilient flooring is that they find it too shiny. Well, Armstrong has used this property as an artistic tool, creating the optical illusion of matte and shine within a pattern.

This is definitely a product that you choose because you like it and not because it's a cheap alternative to other flooring products. The square yard price is around $40. But if you really start to customize your designs, then expect the labor costs to increase by about 30 percent.

Installation

This product requires a specially trained mechanic. There are a lot more seams with this floor because of its ability to customize. And believe me, you do not want to skimp on this part of the job. Make absolutely sure the installer has worked with this product before and has been trained by the manufacturer. The basic subfloor and overall technique is the same as for the others.

Tile, Marble, Stone, Slate, Etc.

At one time, there seemed to be only a few choices within this category that were really affordable. But today, there are an overwhelming number of varieties. This is one area that has truly benefited from the global marketplace. There are fantastic products available that are durable, easily maintained, have incredible character, and will last the lifetime of your home.

If you are working with a budget of $10 to $15/ square foot, you will have some solid choices. There are even some great 8- by 8-inch tiles available for $8/ square foot. And as far as I'm concerned, the Italians have the best designs available. Italian design is classic in style. They do not follow fads, and everything seems to be planned for long-term use.

One of my pet peeves is that most people never get an opportunity even to properly explore all the wonderful options available with these hard surfaces. The reason is that most builders and remodelers don't know enough about the subject. As a result, they usually have a very small selection of "standard" tiles to choose from. If you decide to not use one of the samples they have, then the allowance or budget that the builder gives is completely unrealistic. Most builders use $7/square foot as their basic budget. And usually the consumer doesn't know any differently until they've already signed on the dotted line. It can be very frustrating, especially for me, as a designer. Anyway, that's one of the reasons I was motivated to write this book. To make you, the consumer, better educated.

TILE

The first thing to understand about tile is that every tile is made for a specific purpose. You can't just go pick out the prettiest thing you can find and then decide to use it on your floors, wall, or whatever.

There are specific tiles for walls, floors, residential areas, commercial use, and so on. The following is a floor tile rating chart. This is just a guideline, not a guarantee.

Class 1—Residential bathroom floor only
Class 2—All residential uses except kitchen, steps, and other heavily
        used areas
Class 3—All residential and light commercial
Class 4—All residential and most commercial
Class 5—Unglazed tiles, color throughout body

In addition to the above, there is an entire class of tile that is made just for walls.

Options

As I said earlier, there are an overwhelming number of choices when it comes to tile. The first thing to decide is your budget. How much are you willing to spend? That way you can narrow the field of choices down to something manageable.

Basically, you should be able to choose virtually anything you want in a floor tile for under $20/square foot. An average tile costs around $10 to $12/square foot; a gourmet tile will cost around $14 to $18/square foot; and a handmade tile could cost almost anything depending on the uniqueness of the creator.

Glazed Tile. Glazed tile is exactly what it sounds like; a tile that has a glazing or shine. This is the best choice for maintenance, durability, price, and selection. There are many different styles within this category. Glazed tile is also less expensive than stone or marble, but is perceived to be equal in quality by most people.

Glazed tiles are a breeze to maintain because the finish is baked on. There is no need to seal or wax this tile. Generally, all you have to do is vacuum it with the soft brush attachment of your vacuum. And when it really needs it, damp mop. I've found that if I wipe the floor with a dry cloth as I damp mopped, it becomes much cleaner and never has a dull finish.

The most popular and best choice is to use as large a tile as you can. Why? Because it means less grout and less labor for installation, and it creates the illusion of a larger space. Over the past few years, 12- by 12-inch tiles have become the most popular. But the 16- by 16-inch tile is the fastest growing size today, especially in the South, where tile is far more popular than wood as a flooring choice. And yes, it is appropriate to use large tiles in small spaces. Larger-scale tiles are especially effective for open floor plans.

People in the North seem to think that tile is cold. Well, it is to an extent. However, if it is exposed to the sun through windows or sky-lights, it actually is a great conductor of heat. And it can reduce heating costs by providing radiant solar heat.

My last home was a passive solar one (which means no moving parts were used, only passive heat collectors like water and tile), and ceramic tile was part of my heating system. I used a Mexican tile throughout the living space, the kitchen, and the foyer. It was wonderful and never cold. Another good option for using tile in colder climates is to actually install a heating system in the floor itself. This is a wonderful choice and makes a lot of sense. Of course, you can always resort to wearing slippers!

Unglazed Tile. Obviously this is the opposite of glazed tile. And as a result, it is extremely porous, which means it will stain! I do not recommend this as a choice when there are so many other cost-effective options available.

Installation

At one time there was only one way to install a ceramic tile floor. And that was called a *wet-bed* installation. This meant that a layer of wet cement is put down under the tile. However, technology has advanced, and as a result, this technique is not used very much anymore.

The most common technique today is installing a *cementatious board* as subflooring. This is available in both 1/4- and 1/2-inch thicknesses.

The best option is to install tile directly on top of a concrete floor. So if your home is built on a slab rather than over a basement, it has the perfect base for this type of tile. Of course, if you have a basement, then this tile is also a good choice as a floor surface if you plan on finishing your basement.

The most important aspect of the installation is the installer himself. And if you have read the previous chapters of this book, I am certain you know what I am going to say next. The mechanic who installs your floor makes all the difference in how it turns out. I do not care how much money you spent on the tile, if you skimp on the installation, you will regret it!

Grout. This is obviously a big part of the job. And unfortunately, this is an area in which people make a common mistake. They choose the wrong color of grout! Actually, it's not all the consumer's fault. In my opinion, and the opinion of my tile expert, there should only be *one* choice when it comes to grout color—natural gray! If only natural gray was used, most problems with grout would be eliminated. Never, ever, *ever* use white grout! Even if your tiles are white. Unless you never plan on walking on or washing your white-grout floor. Even if you are willing to seal and reseal white grout every six months, it will eventually end up looking gray. So why not start with gray to begin with and save yourself all that time and aggravation?

Complaints

Cracked Tiles. Tiles should not crack! That is, unless you drop a Mack truck on them. If your tile is cracking and you haven't dropped a heavy object on it, then it either was not properly installed or you chose the wrong kind of tile for the specific application. The only other reason for cracking is if there has been extreme movement in the building itself.

"It's Hard." You're right, it is hard. But the fact of the matter is that most people do not stand for hours on end. If for some reason you will need to stand on tile all day, then wear a good pair of sneakers and relax.

MARBLE

Because of technology, this beautiful product can now be used in many places where it was prohibitively heavy or too difficult to install. Most of the marble used today is only 3/8 inch thick. This is because technology has given us the ability to cut it very thin. This has made marble more affordable and also far easier to install.

But it is for the very same reason that the use of this product is now actually falling off in popularity—at least in the ³/₈-inch thick, 12-by 12-inch size. Do I sound like I'm contradicting myself? Let me explain.

Marble suddenly became available in virtually every tile store. And as a result, salespeople found themselves selling a product they knew very little about. They assumed that since it was installed just like tile, it must be just like tile. Well, it's not!

First of all, it is a porous natural product. Which means it stains. Second, it has a polished surface. Which means it scratches. Third, it needs to be repolished every so often, depending on use. And fourth, it is very, very slippery, especially when wet! Unfortunately, the salespeople didn't have all this knowledge, and therefore didn't give this information to the consumer. As a result, marble was chosen for a lot of applications where it should never have been used. Almost everyone has heard of someone who has had a "marble nightmare." Because of this, the market has gone flat!

All and all, there is a place for marble. But not in heavily trafficked areas.

Pricing

Marble falls between tile and stone in price. Basically, you can either do your foyer floor in marble or you can use ceramic tile in your foyer, bath, and kitchen for the same price.

Installation

This is virtually the same as the installation technique for ceramic tile, with one exception: I recommend using very tiny grout lines. Marble looks best when installed very tightly.

STONE

This is one of the fastest growing areas of flooring. The reason is that stone has such character. It is rich looking and easy to maintain, and durable enough to last a lifetime. It is also suitable for any design style. It is truly understated elegance.

The most popular style is a *tumbled and distressed* finish. This is not a polished floor, but it will develop a natural *patina* (a matte sheen) with use. It has a real "Old World" look. It is usually ³⁄₈ inch thick and available in 16- by 16-inch tiles. Price varies a lot.

One of the advantages of stone is that it can be taken right into the shower. There is no need to change materials if you are using it in a bathroom. However, if you are using this type of installation, make sure there are matching bullnose edges available for the specific stone you have chosen. Bullnose edges are matching curved pieces used for the finished exposed sides of the tile.

Many of these wonderful stones are also available in an *unfilled format*. This means they have some natural pores or holes. These will be filled with grout during installation. Again, I highly recommend using only natural-gray-colored grout. Trust me, it works with virtually any color tile.

Limestone

This is an incredibly interesting look. I love it. Again, do not expect a highly polished product. This too can be considered "understated elegance."

The price ranges from $20 to $40/square foot and the thickness varies from ³⁄₈ inch to 1 inch. Make sure you plan for a transition from this floor to other surfaces in your home, as there is bound to be a variation in thickness. This can be accomplished with a reducer strip, which will level the difference.

This is an extremely porous material. The degree of porosity will vary from one limestone to another. And I cannot stress the importance of a good sealer enough. Limestone must be properly sealed and probably will need to be resealed! There is an incredibly wonderful sealer on the market, Porus Plus by Miracle Sealants. I warn you, it is outrageously expensive—around $200/gallon—but it is worth it! Far better to spend more now on a sealer than to regret your "economy" later when you have stains that have completely ruined the look of your floor.

Installation. Because this is a natural product with a lot of variance in color and sometimes shape, it is up to the mechanic to determine exactly where an individual piece will look and fit best. So it is important to choose an installer wisely. Most stone masons, or stone installers, were first apprentices who worked their way up to working alone. That way they had an opportunity to develop the artistic side of the job. Do not let just anyone install a floor as expensive as this one. It takes a real artist to do it right.

Slate

This is another area that has truly benefited from global marketing. As recently as five years ago, there were only two options available for slate. Today, there is slate from China, Africa, England, India, and Germany. The English variety is particularly elegant.

The price has also become very affordable. Slate starts as low as $15/square foot. I think that's a bargain!

Recognize that this is a *natural* product, and as a result, it too will need to be sealed.

Installation. Slate is installed in much the same way as other stone flooring, using a basic strong foundation. The width of the grout lines can vary based on your individual preference.

Shopping Notes

Take your time. Take a few samples home. Put them on the floor in the room where you plan on using them and walk past them throughout the day, under different kinds of light. Natural light, incandescent light, and fluorescent light can give three different color renditions of the same floor.

You can get a bargain on closeouts, when either a product is being discontinued by the manufacturer (because of the introduction of new patterns) or the retailer is making room for new products.

Look for the brand name—it is usually stamped on both the front and back of the product. Ask for the manufacturer's recommended guidelines for installation and maintenance and the warranty.

We all want the convenience of one-stop shopping, but realize that sometimes this means sacrificing an expert's advice for convenience. This is especially true when it comes to marble and stonework. The global market has made it possible for the one-stop store to carry the product, but this does not mean these retailers are experts when it comes to installation and understanding the proper use of the product.

When choosing a floor, whether tile or stone, choose something that is mottled or shaded. It will hide dirt and stains and be much easier to maintain and live with.

Words of Wisdom

At one time, vinyl flooring used an *asbestos* backing. Because of environmental concerns, this is no longer used. If you have an old floor and you plan on replacing it, *do not* remove the old floor unless you are absolutely positive it is not asbestos. You see, there is no danger from the asbestos unless you expose it. The best bet is to put a new subfloor over the old floor and start anew. If this is not an option, then use a liquid leveling agent on top of the old floor and install the new floor over it.

Yes, you can use a larger-scale pattern in a small room. It will create an optical illusion. The larger the pattern, the larger the room looks. The more tiny pieces that you optically chop a room into, the smaller the room looks!

TCHOTCHKES!

So, what exactly is a tchotchke? The first time I heard the term, I also wondered. I was on my first full-time job as a designer. My new boss asked me to get some tchotchkes for a new china cabinet that had just been delivered. I had no idea what this person was talking about. I assumed it was some technical design term that I somehow had managed not to learn. Well, after everyone had a good laugh, at my expense, they informed me that *tchotchke* was a Yiddish term for accessories!

Accessories are such small items, and they are so important. The best way for me to explain the importance of accessories is to use the example of the little black dress. It doesn't matter how expensive the dress, or how big a name the designer has, the dress still needs to be accessorized with jewelry! The same is true for your room. You can have the perfect sofa, chair, and tables, but unless you add the final touches, it will not look *finished.*

The word *accessory* is all-encompassing. Almost anything can be classified as an accessory: artwork, books, plants, photos, sculptures, flowers, cups, baskets, magazines, dishes, pillows, afghans, throws, teapots, vases, even stationery! About the only thing that doesn't work is the kitchen sink! Although, I guess if I had to, I could make that work.

What makes all these things work well as accessories is what you do with them. A term for best describing how to display accessories properly is *merchandising.* Have you ever noticed how great things look in photo ads, or displayed in stores? They call this merchandising and they teach it in design school. Ultimately, much of it is instinctive. Think about what you do when decorating for a special occasion, such as a birthday party or a holiday. Christmas is a good example. Ever notice how bare the house looks after you take down all the Christmas decorations? Some people have a flair for it and others don't, but that doesn't mean you are hopeless if it's not instinctive. I will do my best to give you some basic rules to make this process doable, even for the least artistic person!

When accessorizing a wall, start by deciding what will be your dominant or *focal element*. This should be the first piece set in place. Either the center or a side position will work. Everything else that you choose for this composition should be complementary. Never attempt to have two focal points. This will just confuse the eye and make it difficult to balance. Balance is extremely important in the composition. When working with symmetrical spaces, attempt to use symmetrical accessories. For example, if you have two bookcases, with windows between them, try using identical baskets filled with dried baby's breath flowers for the base. Then add matching accessories as you work your way up the shelves. Not everything has to be identical. Nevertheless, the overall shape and size and types of elements should be alike.

Besides *symmetrical* balance, there is *optical* balance. Optical balance refers to a composition that does not contain identical elements. In simple terms, the optical weight or appearance of the elements must balance. Pretend you're using a scale—if your wall composition leans one way or another, then you need to work on making things more equal in weight. Remember, this is optical weight, not physical weight! A large painting with a cabinet beneath it can optically weigh the same as a tall secretary. A small painting with a small basket beneath it will not optically weigh the same. Get the picture?

Color and texture will also affect the composition. Some colors optically weigh more than others. The tonal strength of a darker object against a light wall will weigh more than a pastel object against a pastel wall. Another consideration is the wall itself. If you have a strong-patterned wallpaper with highly contrasting colors, then you must consider it in the composition of the elements. Never use small delicate items against a strong wallpaper. They just don't belong together.

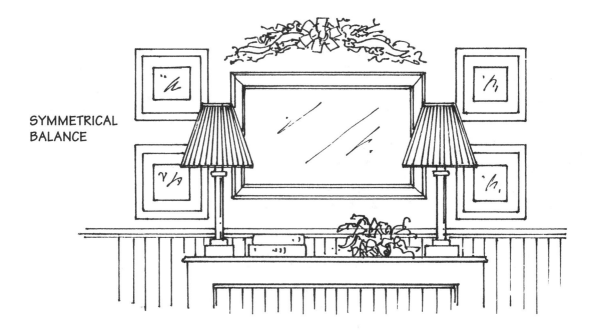

There needs to be a relationship in size, height, color, and interest in order for balance to be accomplished.

Balancing your vertical elements with horizontal elements is important also. The classic traditional or formal design style dictates that you never use diagonals. They disturb the equilibrium. This makes sense when you look at traditional rooms. They are simple in design, usually rectangular, with balancing architectural elements on opposite walls such as windows or doors opposite windows and doors. Another traditional rule of thumb is that ovals and rectangles are preferable to spheres and squares.

Contemporary or informal styles are freer. The design plans are usually irregular, with large windows taking up most of the wall space. This makes them perfect for breaking all the rules of traditional design structure. Horizontal division of a wall is almost never done in contemporary design unless it is necessary for the placement of built-ins or some other logical reason. Using diagonals in composition will create an illusion of undefined space. The eye perceives this as "more space."

FORMAL

So this is perfect for use in smaller spaces to create the illusion of a larger room.

As a designer, once out of school, I began to break many of the rules. Obviously, if a client wanted a pure period room, then I obeyed all the design rules. But what I often discovered is that just because someone was living in a traditional home did not mean that she wanted to decorate it in a traditional style. So I often use more contemporary ideas in traditional spaces. Diagonal placement is a good example of this. This technique works well in both the composition of wall accessories, and the placement of furniture. I'll discuss this later in the chapter on floor plans.

Accessorizing has always been what I consider the most enjoyable part of a design project. After all the hard work is finished, I get to play! The furniture is in place, the windows are dressed, and usually the client is quite happy at this point. The day before accessorizing, I select virtually every possible accessory I think is appropriate for the room, and then load them into the van. Some clients who have not worked with me before get a little nervous when I show up with a truckload of accessories. But they soon relax when they realize that they are not required to buy everything! The real fun begins when I start placing and rearranging accessories all over the room. When the

INFORMAL

client is happy with the selection, I hang all the artwork (a job most people despise!) and place each piece properly, thinking of balance and style. When I leave, everything is picture perfect! Obviously, this is not possible for everyone, but you can accomplish the same thing with a little help.

First, begin by removing all the existing accessories from the room. That also includes lamps and artwork, if there is more than one option for placing these items. Your room should look bare! Now give yourself a little time to get used to this. I want you to be able to see the space as it really is, not as you've grown accustomed to seeing it. This is more difficult than you think. When you are used to something being in a certain place, seeing the space without it is very strange. If you can afford the time, leave the room naked for a few days.

During those few days, gather all the accessories, tchotchkes, and stuff you've been hiding in the closets, basement, and attic. Now clean all this stuff up. Wash, polish, or dust as needed! You will be amazed how much more attractive something is when it's clean!

Next, raid your photo albums and boxes. I want you to find pictures of favorite memories, people, and pets. You will be surprised at how seeing pictures of favorite times can improve the disposition of your room and your mood. Now put all these wonderful memories into frames. There are many beautiful inexpensive frames available in craft and discount stores and through mail-order catalogs. Choose a basic theme for your frames that will match your overall style. For example, try using a variety of gold frames. They can vary in style from fun to formal, but if they are all in gold tones, they will blend well and look interesting.

Okay, now I want you to look for containers. Find baskets, bowls, vases, boxes—anything of that sort. Now, grab a boxful of books and you're ready to get started!

The next step is to analyze your personal accessory style. You need to recognize whether you like a lot of clutter or prefer a cleaner, more open look. If your preference is busy clutter, then you will probably like the look of using a combination of large and small accessories. However, if you tend to like a cleaner, more Spartan look, then it's best to stay with larger accessories.

Now look around your room and decide what surfaces most need something to jazz them up. Don't just look at the horizontal surfaces (tabletops, etc.), but consider the vertical surfaces as well. Try to imagine that you are looking at a photo of the space. This is another great way to get an unbiased perspective of your room and the spaces within it. Often, I have used an instant camera to take pictures inside a client's house. It is an excellent objective way to see what areas of a room need the most work.

Basically, you have a choice of two types of composition. You can either use a group of items that are nearly identical, like a collection of cups, or an arrangement of various items.

If you choose to use various items, begin composing the elements that will be used as accessories by looking at both the vertical and horizontal space, then work on them simultaneously. If one side is next to a wall, then that will be the side you use the tallest item on. This

IDENTICAL COMPOSITION

can be placed either in the vertical or the horizontal plane—a picture or a lamp, or a tall vase or floral arrangement. Any tall item will work.

Then begin working with pieces of declining heights. Perhaps a selection of books, some placed on their sides, others standing upright. Add a small crystal statuette to sit on the top of the books that are not standing. Try to use elements of differing materials. I try to use at least one item that is organic in nature, such as a plant, a basket, or an interesting piece of driftwood. By alternating heights and materials, you can create an inspiring picture. Stacking and varying the placement of objects from front to back will also keep it creative.

The second style of display is to use many of the same kinds of items. For example, one of my clients had a great number of teapots.

VARIED
COMPOSITION

Originally, they were placed sporadically throughout the home. I gathered them together and placed them above the cabinets in the kitchen. Suddenly, it became a *collection*—something to be admired. This idea can work with nearly any repetitive item. Candlesticks, baskets, boxes, *anything* can be presented as a treasured collection.

Once you have repeated this process throughout your room, you will have a good idea of what size and shape of accessory would be most appropriate for each space. You may decide that some specific items need to be replaced. Now that you have a better idea of the size and overall shape needed, you can shop intelligently for the right elements.

Accessories can really set the tone for a room. By using a theme in your choice of accessories, you can truly affect the style of the entire room. If you have basic furniture, you can make the room more formal or informal. Change the look from French country to American country with just a change in accessories. Often, by just rearranging or changing the accessories in a room, you will feel as though you have redecorated the whole room.

Most of us don't realize how much our environment affects us. Adding white cut-

SHELF DECORATION

lace table runners to the kitchen table, for example, can affect your whole disposition. I know that I need lots of natural sunlight. So when planning my own home, I made sure the rooms I would spend the most amount of daytime in would be the most exposed to sunlight during the hours I was there. My kitchen and living room (great room) are filled with brimming sunlight.

You may want to consider changing accessories with the seasons. In winter, I usually use warmer table accessories and green plants. When spring arrives, so does my desire for brighter, lighter, accessories such as flowers and lace table cloths. Experiment for yourself. If something lifts your mood, then use it. It doesn't matter what your mother or your neighbors think. What is important is what *you* think!

Here's an example of an experiment that worked for one of my clients. She had just moved into a new home and was desperate to make it look just right for a home-warming party. However, she didn't have the time or the money at that point to purchase new furniture. So together, we raided every place in the house we could find. I took two spare beds that had no head- or footboards, and I used them as sofas on either side of the fireplace. Then I found a daybed in the guest room and used it as a third sofa against a wall. We continued by adding several chairs, none of which matched. We used spreads and throws to cover each bed, and added lots of pillows. Then we started hanging every piece of "artwork" we could find. I hung real artwork, fake artwork, her children's artwork, even an impression of her son's hands that he had just done in finger painting class. The room had tall ceilings, so I just kept working my way up the walls, filling them entirely. When we finished, it was terrific—the old combined with the new to create the perfect cozy and practical atmosphere the client wanted.

We filled the room with plants, a few candles, and glass work, and it took on the appearance of an artist's studio. When the time came that the client could afford to redo this quick fix, she chose to keep what we had done and just tidy it up with new custom-made slipcovers for the beds, and new covers for the pillows. We added interesting trims and her husband added some real art to our artwork collection. Each time he purchases a new piece of art, they call and ask me to come help them choose a place to hang it. The point is, don't be afraid to try something new. You may find you really like it!

The biggest mistakes most people make is using elements that are too small and/or are all the same size, particularly in big open spaces.

It is important to recognize the proportion and scale of the furniture in your room and to match them with the scale or proportion of the accessories. You must also consider the height of your ceiling. If your ceiling is 9 feet or higher, you will want to use larger-scale accessories for your vertical wall space.

UFOs—Unidentified Floating Objects!

One of my biggest pet peeves is artwork that is hung too high! The rule of thumb is that artwork and mirrors should be hung at eye level. The problem is that eye level is different with each person. My husband is 6 foot 4 and I'm 5 foot 2—exactly whose eye level should we use? Therein lies the problem with *that* rule of thumb! So . . . hang artwork in relation to the surrounding elements. For example, if you are placing a picture above a sofa or table, then hang it so it looks as if it has a spatial relationship with the sofa or table. In other words, hang it 3 to 6 inches above the piece of furniture. If you feel as though you need more height above the picture to draw the eye up, then add additional elements above it. You can use another piece of artwork, a floral display, an architectural element—any number of things will work. The key is that everything looks as though it's part of the same composition and not floating in space by itself.

So many newer homes have wonderful high and vaulted ceilings. They expand the visual and vertical space. But they also can create a visual problem with the furniture. Sometimes matching the proportion of the furniture to the height of the ceiling is difficult. Ceilings can dwarf furniture in the space created between them. One solution is to use large artwork pieces to fill vertical space. Another solution is to divide the vertical wall space visually by using moldings and/or borders. For example, you can use several different stock moldings to create larger, more ornate moldings. These can be placed 8 or 9 feet from the floor. The space above the molding can be painted a different color—by using a color a few shades darker, you can visually bring the space down to an appropriate size for the rest of the room. If you choose, you can accessorize above the molding or you can leave it blank. The contrasting color provides enough interest, without adding accessories.

While on the subject of pet peeves and UFOs, let me vent a little

RIGHT WAY

WRONG WAY

more! Chandeliers are another one of those elements that for some reason end up floating in the ionosphere. A chandelier should be hung so that when you are seated, you can see the faces of your dining party—around 28 inches from the top of the table. The chandelier should just clear your heads. An exception to the rule is if your centerpiece is extremely tall—then obviously you will need to accommodate its height.

Speaking of relationships, some accessories just do not belong together. As with furniture styles, some can be mixed and work well together, and others cannot. American country does not work with Italian Provincial under any circumstance. If something looks out of place, it probably is! Maintain consistency in your elements. If you love handcrafted country items, then use only handcrafted country items. If you attempt to add a highly styled formal piece, it will not work. Find another room or space for it.

Changing your format or feeling from room to room is appropriate. You may choose to have a formal living room, but your kitchen can be more informal. This will allow you to use more homey accessories in the kitchen.

Finding the Right Stuff

The largest resource for the home fashions industry is found in High Point, North Carolina. Twice a year manufacturers from all over the world invade High Point for the furniture show! It is an unbelievable event that no one could possibly cover entirely. What is interesting is that at least half of everything shown is accessories. It is amazing!

As a designer, I really am a professional shopper. Can you imagine a better job than that? I get to go shopping with other people's money! Well, the truth is, I am purchasing with the intention that a specific item will be exactly right for a specific client. But occasionally, even I can make a mistake.

Accessories are usually my most targeted area at High Point. Why? Because it is actually fairly simple to choose furniture from a catalog, but it is impossible to choose accessories that way. Accessories are such a visual art form that it is very difficult to determine if a specific item will work in a specific place unless you can actually see them together.

The High Point show is not an option for consumers; it is an industry show. So where can you go shopping for all these wonderful items? There are several options. Historically, furniture stores have been and still are a great resource for accessories. After all, they are in the business of merchandising furniture. And to make their furniture look good, they use accessories. There are also more and more specialty stores opening every day. And of course, interior design studios often have a large selection to choose from.

Don't be afraid to take several items home, just to try them out. You will probably have to pay for them with a credit card or check until you return them, but it is worth it. Also, don't be afraid to ask if the retailer will help accessorize your home. Many stores will send a designer to your home and then allow him or her to select the appropriate items. If you are purchasing from them, there is usually not a fee associated with this service.

Look for new and interesting places to shop. Art shows, craft fairs, antique shops, even auctions can be great resources. I particularly like to use architectural elements, such as pieces of molding or scrolls. Recently a new antique elements store opened near me. It sells pieces from old buildings—a lot of larger items, such as doors and windows, but also some smaller interesting pieces. A collection of old crystal doorknobs could be the perfect display in just the right place!

Try an antique clothing store. You may discover a collection of old hats to hang on a wall in your bedroom. Or perhaps a collection of antique baby shoes to display on a shelf in a guest room. The idea is to keep an open mind and not to be afraid to experiment.

One of the most often asked questions is how much should I expect to spend on accessories? Obviously, if you intend to begin collecting artwork for investment purposes, then you better have an extensive budget. But for the sake of budgeting the overall cost of decorating a room, I recommend to clients that they should expect to spend approximately 25 percent of the total cost of furnishing the room on accessories. This is the same figure I use when decorating a model home for a builder. This assumes that there are no accessories to begin with. It will provide for print-quality artwork that is well framed. And it will also include artificial plants, lamps, and a lot of other tchotchkes! This will at least give you some idea of what to expect to spend in order to properly finish your room.

Of course, if you are a really good shopper, there are always bargains to be found. Recently I purchased a beautiful handmade wooden birdcage. I found it at an outlet store—-the cost, $58. Two weeks later, a mail-order catalog arrived in my mailbox. The same birdcage was shown at a cost of $199. One of my personal shopping rules is that unless what you want is a one-of-a-kind item, wait a while to shop around—you're almost certain to find it elsewhere. And at least that way, you will have a comparison price.

If you are, however, expecting to have an expert such as a designer make a house call, then don't expect to bargain shop unless you are willing to pay for the designer's time separately.

Don't feel as if every single space in a room has to be filled. Leave some white space. This will allow the eye to find what you want it to see. If you have ever had the experience of going into a store that was so crammed with stuff that you couldn't find anything, then you understand the need for white space.

Also, by leaving some breathing room, you allow yourself the pleasure of buying wonderful treasures when traveling. You never know when you will find an irresistible memento. I love buying symbols of good times. I started a birdhouse collection a few years ago. Now when I travel, I try to find a handcrafted birdhouse that is indicative of the place I am visiting. This combines the fun of collecting with wonderful memories of the places I travel. If I can, I try to seek out the artists or craftsmen who make the pieces. I enjoy hearing their stories, which add a wealth of meaning to their art.

Ultimately, your home should be a reflection of you and your family. Your treasures should be displayed in a way that expresses your life and pleases you. If your favorite chair doesn't match your favorite lap blanket, just call your style "Eclectic French," and you'll be envied for your fashion savvy!

INTERIOR PLANNING—WHERE DO I BEGIN AND DO I NEED AN INTERIOR DESIGNER?

So, do you need a designer to decorate your home? The answer depends on you, your lifestyle, time constraints, and confidence level. Ultimately, the same issues and decisions will need to be addressed with or without the help of a professional. So let me help you understand the process and the stages of development in making your home a true reflection of you.

I have referred several times to the term *design process*. This is a function of design and composition. *Design* is a way of ordering both the visual and the emotional balance in a space. It consists primarily of the elements of form, color, materials, space, and light. It uses the principles of balance, contrast, harmony, proportion and scale, and rhythm.

Composition comes from the Latin word *componere* and means "to put together." It is the organization of the elements of design in a harmonious fashion, following principles for guidance. Sometimes these principles are strict, as in pure period design, and other times they are freer, as in contemporary design. Think of your room as a painting. It is the combination of the above components that creates a beautiful painting. The same is true for interior design. The ultimate goal is to combine function with form. I believe this is what separates designers from engineers. The goal of an engineer is function. A designer believes that having both function and form is possible!

The goal is a functional design that not only looks right, but feels right. A combination of different textures, shapes, and color, in proper scales and balance, will accomplish just that!

First Things First

Developing a "big picture" is important, but to create this, you must first break down your expectations of each individual room and its requirements. Some rooms at first glance seem simple—you expect to sleep in your bedroom—but you may also want to watch television, read, work on your computer, exercise, or iron (yes, for some strange reason, this has become our favorite place to keep an ironing board in my own house!). By making a task list for each room, you will make the planning process easier. In the first chapter, I gave a long list of questions to get you started in the right direction. Begin by putting together a list of your own of all the tasks you envision happening in each room. As you work on each individual room, you may find it impossible to accomplish everything you had hoped. By setting priorities with your wish list, you can expedite the process of elimination as needed.

The Floor Plan

This is the most important part of the design process. It is the basis for everything you will do or purchase for a room. A floor plan is simply a bird's-eye view of your room. Sometimes the ideal plan from a functional point of view is not necessarily the most visually satisfying. Take heart—with the proper selection of colors and textures, almost any plan can be made attractive. First, decide which things that you already own must be placed in this room. Perhaps it is an heirloom desk, or maybe a cherished painting. Knowing what must be used in a room gives you a priority in drawing the floor plan.

The key to a good floor plan is balance. Remember the two different dimensions that you need to consider everywhere: *physical balance* and *optical balance*. In other words, you want to be sure that the arrangement of high and low furniture, combined with the high and low architectural elements (windows, doors, fireplace, etc.) is balanced. You don't want your furniture to look like a line of railroad cars, all lined up with no place to go.

The next step is measuring the space itself. It is not enough to just measure the walls. You have to measure the space and placement of each window, including how far from the floor it is. Measure the placement of any light switch, thermostat, heat register, or any other element that is immovable. We must now transfer this information to a drawing. The easiest scale to work in is $1/4$ inch. This means that each foot in the measurements of your room will be represented by a line of $1/4$ inch in your drawing. For example, if you have a 4-foot space, you will draw a line 1 inch long. Using a ruler, converting it is simple. For the drawing, don't worry about getting any closer than 6 inches to the actual measurements in your room. You can purchase $1/4$-inch scale furniture templates at any office or art supply store. These are thin plastic cutouts of furniture shapes already scaled down to the $1/4$-inch size. You only need one all-purpose template, which can be used to create shapes and sizes similar to your furniture. My favorite has a couple of different-sized sofas, beds, a piano, tables, and a few chairs. I just interchange the shapes and sizes for what I need.

Focal Point

Before you can begin to lay out the floor plan, you must decide the focal point of the room. Sometimes this is obvious, such as a fireplace or a spectacular view of the ocean. Other times, the arrangement of the furniture must create a focal point. If there is a fireplace and a television in a room, I do my best to get the television in the same vicinity as the fireplace. In a family room, whether we like it or not, the television *is* a focal point. Architecturally, though, the fireplace is the focal point. By combining both on the same wall, you can have the best of both worlds, a cozy fire *and* a movie on a cold winter night.

If there is not an architectural focal point, then you must choose an item or area of the room to be the center of attention. A wall system, a conversation area, or even a game table can be the focus of the room, particularly in a family room. In a bedroom, the bed is always the focal point. Even a fireplace should come in second to the bed. Usually there is only one place for the bed, so it makes it easy.

Now it's time to establish the placement of the larger and/or more important items. If you have a piece of furniture that is large or cumbersome, there may be only one place in the room where it fits. If this is the case, obviously, this is where your floor plan will begin. If you own a grand or baby grand piano, here is a special note for you. The right side (bow) of the piano, the side on which the lid opens, should face out to the audience, toward the center of the room. I am not sure why, but I find that pianos are placed backward in a lot of people's rooms. Recently I discussed this with a client, and she said she just assumed the movers knew what was right and so she left it as they had placed it.

The remaining pieces of the furniture should be placed according to their respective sizes with the smallest pieces being placed last. In a family or living room, this usually means that the sofa is the next item to be placed. Most floor plans are either symmetrical or asymmetrical, which means either you are placing sofas opposite each other or you are not. Often you will find that it is possible to place a sofa in two or three different spaces. Start with the most logical position. Then attempt to work the rest of the major pieces around it. Try this with the sofa in as many positions as seems practical. By going through this exercise, you will eventually determine the best arrangement for your room.

When placing furniture, be sure to allow for walkways. If your family has a particular traffic pattern that they use to get from one space to another, consider this: how much space is required for a walkway? Did you know that most bathroom doorways are only 28 inches

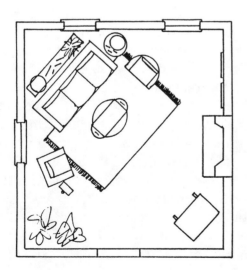 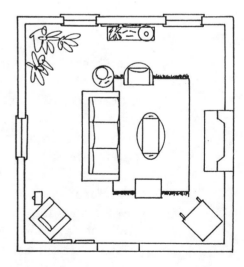

wide? Well, they are, and most of us are comfortable with this width for passage. So, this is the measurement I try to use as my minimum for any walkway or passage area. On occasions, when necessary, I have used as little as 20 inches, but only if the furniture was *low*, so that it does not impair the visual space.

One difficulty associated with laying a room out on paper is that seeing proportions is hard, particularly in regard to height. What may be too small a space on paper can be perfectly acceptable in reality. The reason for this is that our comfort is related to the space that we have at our line of vision. So if nothing is blocking your view at eye level, then you won't feel claustrophobic. If on the other hand, you only have 24 inches of space between two tall pieces of furniture, then you would feel very closed in. I have a very small porch off my kitchen. It is only 6 by 7 feet. On the porch, I have two chairs, a small table, and an ottoman (footstool). There is only 13 inches between the chair and the ottoman to use as a passageway to the door. Because the ottoman is only 17 inches high, it doesn't obstruct my line of vision. So, although it is a small amount of space, it *feels* okay. If on the other hand, I had a taller object 13 inches from the chair, it might feel very uncomfortable.

A common problem is to be stuck with a major piece of furniture that we hate! Sometimes it's one of those white elephants that we purchased ourselves. Other times, Aunt Hilda knew we would just love it, and willed it to us—while she's still living! Whatever the circumstances, sometimes we have to learn to make the most of a bad thing.

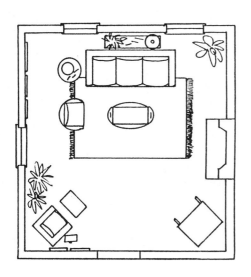

FLOOR PLAN OPTIONS

If you are considering a radical change in furniture, for example, buying a sectional to replace a sofa, you may find it helpful to make a true-size template. I have often used this trick with clients, especially if the new sectional is replacing virtually all other upholstered seating in a room. Use newspaper to cut out pieces that are the same dimension as the sectional. Then by placing the paper on the floor, you can get a very good idea of how the sectional will fit in your room. This allows you to make necessary changes well before ordering.

There are many ways to accomplish this. If it is an upholstered item, then adding a slipcover or throwing a large gorgeous scarf over it can help. But the key to living with the unwanted is not letting it paralyze you until you can afford to change it. Accessories are the world's best camouflage. It is amazing how much better something can look with a picture or a plant on it, or around it.

If it is a large-scale wood piece, such as a cabinet, then open the doors and fill it with pretty things—plants, baskets, brass candlesticks, crystal boxes, anything that you like. If it is a table, then cover it with beautiful accessories. Try your favorite lamp. Family pictures and silk flowers can really make a difference. The biggest obstacle is your point of view. Get your personal focus off the ugly item and concentrate on the rest of the room. Try my photograph idea. Take several pictures of your room, then analyze them. You will be amazed at how seeing a room in a photograph can reorient your focus. This perspective is the best view you can possibly get of your room.

Another consideration for your floor plan is the *relationship* of a piece of furniture with the surrounding furniture and/or accessories. It will make it easier to decide where to place things. If your sofa is the largest piece of furniture in the room, then it will dominate the chair. The chair will dominate a small table. The table acts as a complement to the chair. Plants and other accessories also act as complements to surrounding objects. It is the combination that creates the finished picture. If you can't think of a good reason for a relationship between two pieces of furniture, they probably don't belong together!

A recent article in a professional design journal showed a celebrity living room. In the middle of the living room was a canoe! The written commentary was, "Why not?" The home was rustic in style, so the canoe seemed to fit. As I have said to clients for more than twenty years, my goal is to make them happy. It doesn't matter if I like it.

Clients who are pleased with the way their home looks will recommend me. However, I have to admit that even I have my limits—I have *never* used a canoe in a living room!

Scale and proportion are so important when choosing furniture. The overall dimension and feel or visual weight of the pieces must match. A dainty French Provincial love seat will never be able to balance with a heavy Eighteenth-Century English wing chair. Their overall proportions are far too different. When combining styles or periods, this is the most important feature to be aware of. Considering the scale is also important. For example, if you have a small room, you can use large-scale furniture, but not much of it. Two large chairs would probably look better than a large sofa. The chairs allow for space in between, and space is part of the balance in the overall floor plan.

As I discussed in Chapter 12, color can also affect balance. Stronger colors visually weigh more. So if you have a small room with light-colored walls, do not use large-scale, strongly colored furniture. By choosing a color of similar value and hue to the walls, you can make a large piece of furniture appear smaller. It will become part of the overall picture and not a dominating feature of its own. If, however, your goal is to create a cozy den in rich dark colors, you can accomplish this and still maintain balance with large-scale furniture by choosing deeper, richer colors for both the walls and the furniture. The key is to follow through with the rest of your complementary pieces. You may have to use only a single lamp or side table, but be sure it is heavy in scale, and dark in color. A heavily carved Georgian-style walnut table would be perfect.

What If I Have No Wall Space?

This is a common problem. Many rooms suffer from an overabundance of windows and doors. But this can be wonderful if the room is large enough to allow for the furniture arrangement to be focused toward the center of the room. Placing a pair of sofas in an L-formation in the center of the room and adding tables around it can be a very effective way of accenting this type of space. Then by filling it with artwork, *étagères* (open shelving units), a writing desk, or other complementary pieces in the spaces between the windows and/or doorways, you can accomplish a well-balanced plan.

On the other hand, if your room is small and has no wall space, it can be more of a challenge. Notice I said *challenge*, not impossibility. You must decide what your traffic patterns are and how they will affect the placement of furniture. Placing furniture in front of windows is perfectly fine, as long as you consider this in your overall scheme. If a sofa cannot be centered on the window, then you must virtually take notice of where it will appear in the window. This is important for planning a window treatment. If, for example, you have long side-panel draperies (fabric on either side of the window, with the center left open), the sofa will visually cut off one drapery panel. You will have a very strange, lopsided-looking window treatment. In this case, you would be better to use a window treatment that did not come down to the floor, like a valance treatment with sheers or a shade treatment. This would allow the placement of the sofa as necessary, without interfering with the window treatment.

Placing furniture in front of a patio or sliding doors is also possible, if they are not often used to go in and out of. I suggest you place the furniture at least a foot away from the doors, to give the illusion of a passageway. It also may be enough space to allow you to pass through when you absolutely need to.

One of my clients had a living room with six windows and two doors. In addition, it had a fireplace! She was very frustrated with attempting to arrange this room. The solution was to use a beautiful silk-look fabric, which we shirred (gathered) and used to cover the walls and windows on either side of the fireplace. The fabric went from ceiling to floor, wall to wall, hiding the windows on either side of the fireplace. The fabric used was close in color to the rest of the walls. We hung mirrors on the remaining wall space around and above the fireplace. Suddenly it became a wonderful, elegant space with two walls that could now be used for the placement of furniture. From the outside of the house, it just looked like draperies. The cost was minimal and no permanent change or damage was done.

Did this client *need* an interior designer to accomplish this? You decide. It's not that she could not have done this herself. She just hadn't thought of it. In many situations, this is what a professional can bring to the picture. It is years of dealing with problems and difficult situations that have given us the insight and the creative solutions. So much of what we do is instinctive. It comes with years of practice and training, and most people can learn to do the same thing. Ultimately, it depends on whether you have the time and the resources to do it.

Choosing an Interior Designer

A concern that I have heard expressed is that if you work with an interior designer, the room will end up being a reflection of the designer and not yourself. This could not be further from the truth. Capable, qualified, sincere designers want to make you happy. Of course, a few bad apples spoil the reputation of the industry.

You should know that there is a difference between a *decorator* and a *designer*. Generally speaking, designers have a degree, and decorators do not. Trade associations test the qualifications of prospective members before admitting them. The American Society of Interior Designers (ASID) is the major professional affiliation for designers. It is very strict in its discipline and expects designers to keep up with continuing education. For example, a number of years ago, ASID required me to take a course in designing for the disabled. I had to learn the requirements of the ADA—the Americans with Disabilities Act. I must admit, it was an enlightening course. We were assigned a different disability each day. One day I had to use a wheelchair. The next I had to wear sunglasses with Vaseline rubbed on the inside of the lenses. This simulated low vision or glaucoma. It certainly gave me a different perspective on design, and on life. The point is, a designer who is a member of ASID is a qualified professional.

This does not mean that your personality will match with that of any ASID designer. In working with young designers, I always caution them about personality conflicts. If someone does not like you, it doesn't matter how good a designer he is; he will not be able to please you. It is always a good idea to get recommendations from people you know. ASID publishes a list of affiliated designers by region. To get a copy contact the nearest ASID office. Their headquarters are located in Washington, DC, at 202-546-3480.

The design industry has no regulated method of charging for services, so you may find it difficult to compare price from one designer to another. Individual circumstances will play a big part in how a designer decides on her pricing structure. If a designer has a showroom with furniture displayed in it, there is a good chance that she has open accounts with the manufacturers or suppliers. This allows the designer to make some of her income from the commissioned sale of furniture. However, this will only be true if you purchase your furniture through the designer.

Independently employed designers who do not have direct access to manufacturers usually charge a larger per hour fee. This can range anywhere from $35/hour to $250/hour. Interior designers employed by retail furniture stores work strictly on commission. So it is important that you not work with someone else in the store after you've started dealing with one designer. That could be grounds for the *other* person to demand part of the commission.

It is a common practice for designers to work off a *retainer*. This is the same kind of retainer that the legal profession uses. Many suppliers, particularly if the designer must go through a middle man, require a deposit from the designer. This is the reason for the retainer. But please be careful to secure receipts for any orders you authorize. There have been situations in which furniture was ordered without the client's knowledge. Again, one bad apple can ruin it for everyone.

Because of the diversity of the projects I have worked on, I have found that flexibility is the key to determining a proper fee schedule. If a client is planning on doing all the leg work and shopping, then I usually charge a per hour consultation fee. If however, the client is purchasing everything through me, then I can expect to make a profit on the furniture. In some cases, this will eliminate the need to charge an hourly fee. It all depends on the specific circumstances of the project.

The most important aspect to choosing a designer is *communication*. If for example, the designer thinks she has your permission to purchase an oriental rug for the dining room, she may believe that you mean for her to select *and* order a rug, when you may have *meant* for her to bring a number of options for you to see. In my first meetings with a new client, I repeatedly stress how important it is for them to talk to me. I cannot help if I do not know which lines they are thinking along.

As a designer, I approach a client's home from many different levels and values. I never begin to work on the design process until I am confident that I know the family and their requirements. We must establish a relationship of trust and communication before I can begin to understand the goals of the design project. This is actually the hardest part of my job. The design process itself is nearly second nature to me after twenty years of practice. Certainly all designers do not operate the same way I do. Other designers may approach a project differently and still be effective. You have to be the ultimate judge. If you are comfortable with someone, and you have checked out his credentials, then that should give you confidence in choosing.

Shopping Notes

Never, ever allow yourself to be talked into purchasing anything! If you are not comfortable that it is absolutely the right piece, in the right color, at the right time—do not order it. *Special orders are not returnable!* A special order is anything that is not purchased directly off the showroom floor. Even if you ordered it exactly as shown, it is still a special order.

Be sure to get *all* the dimensions of any furniture you are considering ordering. Check these dimensions against your plan.

Be sure anything you are purchasing will actually fit through doorways and hallways. Sharp turns can be difficult to maneuver.

Making the Right Choices

Accepting the fact that a house is *never* finished will help you to be content with your home.

As we change, mature, and become more complex in our own personalities, desires, and needs, so do our homes. Having one special chair or beautiful armoire can go a long way in bringing us joy and comfort in our home. Learn to relax and enjoy the process of evolution of your life and your family. Remembering that your home is to be of *service* to you, and you are not to be *slaves* to it, will keep your perspective where it should be.

My personal philosophy has been that if I cannot afford what I really want, then I will wait until I can afford it. I refuse to purchase something cheap, just to fill space. I consider this a waste of money. It means, for example, that I may have to be content with a card table and folding chairs for many years before I can afford the dining room I really want—but it is well worth it.

OPPOSITES ATTRACT!

Design school never prepared me for the psychology of people! I had no idea that as an interior designer, I would be providing therapy to clients.

It is amazing how much clients will tell their designer. I get to know my clients on a very intimate basis. After all, I am creating a very special place—their nest—and in the process, their personal life gets exposed! There are almost no secrets kept. I'm in their kitchen, their bedroom, even their closets! And I am definitely privy to the relationships in their life and how they function.

The old saying is true: opposites do attract! The reason is because it makes life more interesting. But it also makes it more difficult to meet the needs and preferences of two people who do not agree!

I've been caught in between two differing partners arguing about finances, wedding planning, bar mitzvahs, educational decisions, and parenting decisions. I've even helped to divide up a household going through a divorce. The couple actually let me decide who got what!

I have had crying wives call for advice on how to deal with impossible husbands. I have had teenagers call for advice about parents. I have been called to solve problems on animal management and vacation planning. Never, ever, did they even discuss this in interior design school!

So how have I dealt with these situations? Usually with humor. But when it came to real interior design or furnishing situations, I figured out some basic rules:

❀ Whoever is actually going to be using a piece of furniture should get to choose. However, the overall aesthetic design and color should be compatible to the rest of the space.

For example, I had a client promise her husband a leather chair and ottoman for his birthday. He was thrilled until he realized that they were mauve (dark pink) leather! But honestly, it was the best choice for the rest of the room. This is a great example of compromise.

❀ If you absolutely cannot agree, then allow an unbiased person to help make the selection.

❀ No one wins all the time! So don't expect to have total control.

❀ Most often, one person cares more than the other about decorating. If that is the case in your home, then let the one who cares the most make most of the decisions. Why? Because he or she will be more involved and take more time making the right decisions than someone who does not care.

❀ Everyone should have at least one space to call his own. That also means he gets to decide what happens there.

❀ There is no such thing as a "perfect" house, a "perfect" piece of furniture, or a "perfect" price!

❀ This is not a matter of life and death—lighten up! Enjoy the ride.

❀ Few things last forever. Don't expect furniture to either.

❀ Be realistic in your choices. Don't try to turn an informal slob into a "formal fancy" by buying formal "no-touch" furniture. You will only end up angry and disappointed. Worse yet, the furniture will probably be ruined. What a waste.

❀ It is possible to find a sofa that a 6 foot 4 man and a 5 foot 2 woman can both use. How? By buying an ottoman to match. That way, you can put your feet up and be comfortable, no matter what your height.

❀ If one of you is a neatnick and the other is not, then organize, organize, and organize! Make it easy to keep things neat. There are so many ways to encourage organization: baskets, storage ottomans, shelving, hooks, and so on!

❀ Always be willing to listen to the other person. Usually, that's more important to someone than actually getting her way, and you'll always benefit from another perspective.

❀ There is always more than one way to accomplish something. Let a professional help you find all your options.

❀ When discussing pricing, it is usually easier for a man to understand costs if you compare them to the price of his car. After all, most men purchase a car more often than furniture. So it is easy to justify price and discuss quality when you compare sofas, for example, to cars. Yes, it is possible to purchase a sofa for $300, just as it is possible to purchase a cheap car. But is that the sofa he is going to want to drive?

❀ If you have no idea how much the total project is going to cost, then sit down with an expert and put together a couple of budgets. It is not difficult for experts to give you low, middle, and high price ranges. By doing this first, you will have fewer disappointments and arguments later.

❀ If you have a tight budget, then you probably think you cannot afford a professional. Well, you are very wrong. A professional can help prevent you from making costly mistakes, which you really can't afford.

❀ Communicate with the one you love. Nothing is more frustrating than going through the process with a couple when one remains mute the entire time. Or worse, when one says, "Whatever you want, honey." And then, when it's delivered, that person says, "I never did like that thing!"

❀ Be honest with yourself. If you are the type of person who gets bored with things fast, then don't spend a fortune on anything! But if you are the kind of person who will almost never change a thing, then go ahead and get the best you can. I spent a fortune on an armoire years ago. It is still my favorite piece of furniture. I waited a long time to buy it, and would never have settled for anything else. But I also know that I will never tire of it. The same is true of my dining room set. I used a cheap card table and folding chairs for years until I could afford what I really wanted.

❀ Be open-minded. You may think you know what you like, but it's quite possible there is something else out there that you haven't even seen yet. Most people have not been exposed to all that is available. There may be something out there that both you and your loved one will end up loving!

Have Fun!

I have spent over twenty years listening, watching, and working with clients on every aspect of their homes. And I have had a great time through most of it. Oh, I hate dealing with problems such as the wrong color fabric showing up, or worse yet, finding out it's been discontinued after everything else for the room has already been completed. But for the most part, I love my job. I love people. And I get the biggest kick out of helping them love their homes.

Learn to accept yourself and your housemates for who they are. Realize that most couples do not agree. And that's okay. Yes, this can be a challenge, but it can be fun. Don't put unrealistic expectations on yourself.

An interesting observation I have made over the years is that most of us become more traditional in our taste as we age (At least until we reach retirement. Then for some strange reason that I have yet to understand, some people go to the absolute opposite spectrum—very contemporary!). So don't be surprised to find your taste suddenly changing. Instead, enjoy and learn to incorporate your newfound style with the old.

The process of decorating should not be a difficult job—it should be an adventure. And just like going out into the unknown world in any other adventure, you may need a guide to help you through it. Many designers are willing to work with you in many different ways. If you feel you want to do all the leg work and just want help in the final decision making, then say so up front. If you want to just sit back and relax and let someone else deal with it all, that can be arranged as well.

Furnishing a home *is* actually a lot of work, but it doesn't have to be drudgery. It should be a pleasant job. It is not a race or a competition. It is an opportunity to explore your dreams, your passions, and your life. Take your time and enjoy it. If you start out with the right attitude and give yourself the time necessary, you will have fun. More importantly, you will have created a place where you will always feel good.

Consider this an opportunity to expand your horizons. It is not necessary that the entire house be finished in six weeks. You may find a whole new you and a whole new style developing as this process goes on. I have thoroughly enjoyed watching a client's level of design sophistication grow as we progress through a home. One family in particular has been working with me for thirteen years. We have done their home over twice and also recently built and furnished a home in the South that will become their retirement home. They have five children, and as the children grew up and left, we redid and readjusted the home to new needs, such as an ailing parent moving in. Through it all, we have become good friends. And they have become very well educated in the home fashion world. As a result, we were able to try more interesting ideas as their security with their own taste and choices grew. In this way, I have been very fortunate to have continuing close and long-lasting relationships with clients.

I wish you the best with your creative journey.

GLOSSARY

Accessories (Yid: tchotchke) • Any item or a collection of items that adds a decorative or stylistic finish to a furniture piece or an area of your home.

American Country • Furniture made during the eighteenth century by traveling cabinetmakers. The construction and details of these pieces are usually crude, simply styled, and are often painted.

Apron • The board or front piece that is placed at a right angle, directly below a tabletop. Better-quality dining table extension leaves have an apron, which allows for a continuous band around the table.

Arm Cover • A hemmed and fitted piece of fabric that covers about a third of the arms of a sofa or upholstered chair.

Arm Sleeve • The same as an arm cover, except an arm sleeve covers the entire arm from front to back, and down the inside to the seat.

Armoire • A large one-piece or multipiece cabinet used for clothing, storage, housing electronics, and the like.

Bleeding • The process of one color running into another during painting or staining, or the appearance of an element such as wood knots underneath a coat of paint.

Box Pleats • A series of pressed folds in a fabric, similar to the pleating style of many women's skirts.

Built-In • A storage system that combines cabinets, drawers, and shelves, often custom-built.

Cape Cod • A compact rectangular home of one-and-a-half stories, usually having a central chimney and a steep sloping roof.

Case Goods • Any piece of furniture that can be used to store things in, such as dressers, desks, bookcases, and cabinets.

Chaise (or Lounge) • A large, usually upholstered modular section for two or more people.

Channel • The aluminum rail of a valance.

Chip Core • A process of wood construction where many small pieces of wood are bonded together to form large sheets of wood. This decreases the possibility of warping and moisture absorption.

Classic • A term applying to an established standard and acknowledged excellence.

Closeout • When a store decides to stop carrying a particular item and marks the price down for sale.

Collection • A set of furniture put together by a manufacturer according to style and price.

Colonial • An American style originating from the Colonial period that is a modified version of English Georgian (or formal English) style.

COM (Customer's Own Material) • Custom-bought fabric for upholstery use.

Contemporary • Any modern, nontraditional, or up-to-date style produced since 1920.

Cording (Welts) • A decorative trim made of strands tied together to create a decorative rope. Welts are cording covered by fabric.

Crown • The slightly arched top side of a seat cushion.

Cut Pile • Any surface of a fabric or carpet that has individual threads or fibers, as opposed to looped pile.

Cutting • A small sample of fabric no more than 3 to 5 inches in length that is cut from the current inventory of a manufacturer, used to determine color compatibility. Also refers to the production of a collection of case goods, which occurs two to four times a year.

Daybed • A sofalike bed consisting of a headboard and a footboard of the same height, with a sideboard running along the back of the bed.

Decorator • An interior decorator who generally does not have a degree in design.

Designer • An interior decorator who possesses a degree in design, and often belongs to a trade association like the American Society of Interior Designers (ASID).

Dimmer • A special switch that dims the lights, enabling one to create different moods through lighting.

DIY • An acronym for "do-it-yourself."

Dominant • The strongest color or colors in a given area. Also refers to the strongest or largest piece of furniture in a room.

Doublefold Shade • A type of shade that is divided horizontally, that can be opened from the top down or the bottom up.

Dovetail • A method of joining two pieces of wood together, often done with drawers. It refers to the wedge-shaped projections on the end that alternate and interlock.

Dowel • A metal, plastic, or wooden strut or pin that is often used for support on furniture such as chairs and stools, as well as in shutters.

Durability • The overall strength of a fabric and its ability to withstand wear over time.

Dustcover • A cover for the top of a valance that aids in keeping out light and dust.

Eastern • Styles influenced by those of the Middle East, India, China, and Japan, ranging from minimalist to highly decorative. Often involves lacquered finishes and natural materials.

Eclectic • A decorating style that combines both traditional or period furniture with more contemporary or modern styles.

Étagère • Standing or hanging open shelves.

Face Weight • The number of ounces of fiber per square yard. The more yarn, the tighter the density and the greater the durability. This also means the higher the face weight, the more expensive the product.

Faux Finish • French meaning "false," a technique of finishing that emulates a texture from nature, such as animal skin or wooden panels.

Focal Element • The central or most dominant point in a room or design.

Formal • A more elaborate or decorative style. When used to refer to period styles, such as Eighteenth Century, the term also means symmetrical or highly organized.

French Country • Eighteenth-Century country furniture that is informal, comfortable, and more universally appealing than its formal Parisian counterparts.

French Provincial • The style of the Louis XV period. Rooms were usually paneled and painted, or covered with fabric wallpaper, or stenciled. Colors were usually delicate and often the walls were set with mirrors. The use of silks, printed cottons, embroidery and hand-painted linens was prevalent.

French Traditional • The more formal style of the Louis XVI period, popular in Paris.

Fullness • The degree of fabric used over the width of a drapery.

Georgian • A style popular during the reigns of George II and George III (1727–1810) in England. Usually embellished with heavy carving.

Glide • The track that a drawer slides on. Available in wood, metal, and plastic.

Groover • A plastic slat with channels on one side that give support to vertical blinds that are made of softer materials, such as cotton.

Hand • The feel, weight, and texture of a fabric.

Hardware • Also known as "pulls," hardware refers to the exterior knobs, handles, and trim used on furniture. These can be wood, plastic, or metal plated.

Informal • A more casual style. This may also refer to contemporary styles.

Ink Blot Test • The selection process I have developed for my clients to help them find their own personal style.

Islander • Usually refers to the style of the Caribbean Islands, where colors are bright and varied; often using louvered shutters instead of windows and screens.

Italian • Styles based upon the designs of the Italian Fifteenth Century; elaborate use of colored marble and architectural trims.

Kiln-Dried • A process of removing excess moisture and sap from wood that prevents warping.

Laminate • A plastic material used to coat fabrics for durability. Also refers to plastic construction material such as Formica.

Leaf • A piece of wood that fits into the top of a dining table to extend it to a larger size.

Light Bridge • A piece of wood that attaches between two tall cabinets. It usually has two or three light fixtures housed in the top. A light bridge can be used over a bed or a cabinet, such as a buffet.

Linter • A by-product of the cotton producing process.

Louvers • Slats of a shutter placed at an angle.

Love Seat (Chair-and-a-Half) • A small sofa with seating for two. A chair-and-a-half is a smaller version of a love seat.

Modular • A sofa made up of several pieces that can be arranged in any fashion.

Mortised • A slot made in a piece of wood in order to join it to another.

Occasional Piece • Small wood furniture, such as end tables, coffee tables, and the like.

Palladian • An arch-topped window.

Passive Solar Heat • A method of heating using nonmotorized materials such as black fiberglass tubes filled with water, or dark-colored ceramic tile that is exposed to sun entering through the windows; the sun heats the tile and as the heat dissipates, it warms the room.

Pattern Matching • The aligning of one piece of fabric along another, so that the pattern or design matches.

Pediments • Originally referred to the triangular shape at the top of Greek temples. Today, it refers to any decorative element at the top of an item.

Period • Formal styles that were so dominant during their time that they have come to define that period.

Pier Cabinet • A tall, narrow cabinet.

Pilling • When a fabric becomes fuzzy instead of maintaining its smooth original appearance.

R-value • A measure of the resistance that an insulating or building material has to heat flow. The higher the number, the greater the resistance.

Rabbeted • A deeply notched groove on a shutter that enables it to be tightly closed, preventing light gaps.

Railroading • A process of applying upholstery fabric to a piece in a side-to-side method, rather than an up-and-down method.

Repeat • The size and frequency of a recurring pattern on wallpaper or a fabric.

Return • The dimension measured from a wall to the front of a drapery on either side.

Reupholster • To redo or change the covering, cushions, etc., on a piece of furniture.

Seconds • Refers to product that does not meet the manufacturer's standards of production, sold at a price lower than normal retail value.

Sectional • A three-piece modular sofa consisting of a corner and two armed sections that fit together in an L-shape.

Sheers • A light, see-through translucent fabric that allows light to filter through it.

Shim • A thin tapered piece of material that is used to fill in a space or gap in order to support, level, or adjust fit.

Shirring • Small pleats or folds, as in a gathered skirt.

Slipcover • A tailored cover that slips over pieces of furniture.

Stability • A term referring to how much stretch or give a fabric has.

Stacking Dimension • How much space a shade or blind requires when it is in the open position.

Stile • The vertical portion of a frame or panel.

Tackless Installation • A method of installing carpet using wood strips with metal grippers, versus using tacks to nail down the carpet.

Tchotchke • See Accessories.

Tester Bed • A bed with tall spindles at the headboard and/or footboard. A tester bed with a covered top on it is called a canopy bed.

Throw • A large, one-piece unit that is literally thrown over a piece of furniture. Unlike a slipcover, a throw is not fitted.

Tones • The relative strength of a color, as in dark versus light hues.

Tongue and Groove • A method used to put up paneling where each piece fits together by means of a fitted slat (the tongue) and a recessed channel (the groove).

Track-Free • A style of carpet that uses different textures within its finish to camouflage footprints.

Traditional • A term universally used for furniture that is not modern or contemporary, usually referring to a more classic style.

Traverse • The ability of a blind to travel vertically or horizontally.

Trompe L'oeil • French meaning "to fool the eye." A painting technique for creating murals that give the impression of more space.

Tufting • An organized series of depressions or indentations in a fabric, created by drawing a thread through and pulling it tight to the back.

Undertones • A subdued color or a color beneath another.

Valance • A horizontal heading or top piece for draperies. It can be made of wood, metal, fabric, or anything your heart desires.

Wet-Bed Installation • A method of installing ceramic tile into a layer of wet cement.

CREDITS

Frank Essis, Essis & Sons Carpet, 1320 Manheim Pike, Lancaster, PA 17601

Gloria Banta, Banta Tile & Marble Co., Inc., 1284 Loop Road, Lancaster, PA 17601

Jeff Gable, Gable Designs, 682 Central Manor Road, Lancaster, PA 17603

Sherry Qualls, Gen. Mgr. Advertising Services, and Thom Cooke, Head Designer, Armstrong World Industries, Inc., 2500 Columbia Avenue, Lancaster, PA 17603